S0-FAL-272

OPPORTUNITIES IN
THE SECURITIES INDUSTRY

Edward O'Toole

VGM Career Horizons
A Division of National Textbook Company
8259 Niles Center Road, Skokie, Illinois 60077

Securities Industry:

Photo Credits
Front cover: upper left and right, NTC; lower left, First National Bank of Chicago; lower right, American Stock Exchange.

Back cover; upper left, *Financial Talk*; upper right, NTC; lower left, First National Bank of Chicago; lower right, American Stock Exchange.

1985 Printing

Copyright © 1981 by National Textbook Company
4255 West Touhy Avenue
Lincolnwood (Chicago), Illinois 60646-1975 U.S.A.
All rights reserved. No part of this book may
be reproduced, stored in a retrieval system, or
transmitted in any form or by any means, electronic,
mechanical, photocopying, recording or otherwise,
without the prior permission of National Textbook Company.
Manufactured in the United States of America.
Library of Congress Catalog Number. 80-80428

5 6 7 8 9 0 BB 9 8 7 6 5 4 3 2

ABOUT THE AUTHOR

Edward O'Toole has been involved in various aspects of the securities industry for several years. He has written several books and articles about the industry. Early in his career, he published *The New World of Banking* and *How to Gain Financial Independence*. Then, for a while, he reported on the stock and money markets for the *New York Times,* including some time he spent as a foreign correspondent for the *Times* with the European financial and investment markets as his assignment. He also is a former managing editor of both *Finance Magazine* and *Mergers & Acquisitions Magazine* as well as the writer of numerous articles on Wall Street for various financial publications.

Mr. O'Toole, who attended both Fordham College and the Harvard Business School, has worked for such securities firms as Dean Witter Reynolds, the Chase Manhattan Bank, Merrill Lynch, and Investors Diversified Services.

Edward O'Toole is a registered stockbroker who has been accredited by the New York Stock Exchange and the Securities and Exchange Commission.

3 1172 01923 5993

CONTENTS

About the Author iii

1. **An Overview of the Securities Industry** 1

    Almost universal in scope. Examples from a coast-to-coast flight.

2. **Wall Street: Plenty of Paradoxes** 13

    Small beginnings. Unique contributions. Riding the crest. The industry comes of age. Steady growth for decades—almost. Effects of World War I. Roaring to disaster.

3. **Wall Street: Between the Acts** 25

    An era of profound change in the industry. Weaknesses leading to the second act.

4. **The Buy Side of the Wholesale Market** 37

    Corporations as buyers of services. The federal government as buyer of services. Municipal government as buyer of services. Institutional investors as buyers of services. A pair of changes.

5. **The Buy Side of the Retail Market** 51
   Reliance upon stockbrokers. Many reasons to buy or sell securities. New types of securities.

6. **The Selling Side of the Wholesale Market** 61
   The rise of securities "supermarkets." A major sell side activity: investment banking. Three actual offerings. A second major area: government securities. Market strategies of the expanded firms. Other income-producing activities.

7. **The Sell Side of the Retail Market** 79
   Change to a buyers' market. Sellers' responses to a buyers' market. Expanded career opportunities.

8. **Modern Securities Firms** 87
   Challenge from a new corner. The large firms: directions and patterns. New developments as change factors. The account executive. Concluding notes on A/E compensation.

9. **Marketplaces and Marketmakers** 109
   Needed: a national market system. Role of the exchanges. Roles of the over-the-counter markets. A game of keep-up. Two questions for the NYSE. What about the future?

10. **Getting Started and Getting Ahead** 129
    Paths of entry. Desirable personal characteristics. Suggested areas to consider. Compensation levels. Placement and advancement of women. Conclusion.

Appendix A: Glossary of Securities Terms 143

Appendix B: For Further Information 149

Overleaf: Wall Street, home of the New York Stock Exchange, has given its name to the securities industry; Wall Street means the center of the investment world. (John Maguire, Matar Studio, Inc.)

CHAPTER 1

AN OVERVIEW OF THE SECURITIES INDUSTRY

For most young people who have not made it a subject of special study, the securities industry is a strange world. On first encounter, it seems to have a language all its own: hedging, voting trust certificate, load and no-load, random walk theory, debenture, puts and calls, Rule of 72, selling short and selling short against the box, wire house, writing naked, and many other terms peculiar to the investment business. There also are many terms in common usage that have a special meaning in the securities industry. Book value, for example, has nothing to do with the value of a book. Principal does not refer to the head of a school. Record date, alas, has an entirely different connotation than an appointment in a discotheque with someone interesting.

Investment jargon, admittedly a mystery to the novice, has its own logic and becomes readily comprehensible to those working in the investment markets. Indeed, the language of the securities world is worth learning whether or not you intend to carve a career on Wall Street. Incidentally, Wall Street is one investment term with a double meaning that is very well known—i.e., the name of an actual street in the heart of the financial district in New York City, and the general label for most of the investment world.

ALMOST UNIVERSAL IN SCOPE

The securities industry is, or should be, of vital interest to everyone since just about everyone in this country has a stake in it. With the possible exceptions of the food, shelter, and clothing industries, the most pervasive economic sectors are the capital markets and the money markets. The capital markets embrace funds committed for relatively long-term use, usually more than a year; the money markets represent short-term investments of a year or less. Together, these markets comprise the core of the securities industry, one of the largest industries in the world's largest economy.

Some 25 million Americans are direct owners of securities issued by approximately 10,000 publicly owned corporations and several thousand government bodies and agencies. Additionally, as many as 150 million individuals have an indirect stake in billions of shares of stock and thousands of debt issues collected in pension funds and other vast pools of securities administered by professional money managers.

The total market value of the financial assets of U.S. individuals invested in securities, including government debt, exceeds $1 trillion. Scientists say $1 trillion may not read like much, but actually it's so large it defies human comprehension unless it's put into a more limited context. For example, if you were to spend $10,000 every sixty seconds, every hour day and night, seven days a week, do you know how long it would take to consume $1 trillion? It would take about two centuries, which is a long time and a lot of money.

People think of the dimensions of the U.S. automotive industry, with an annual sales volume of over $100 billion, as impressive. The sales volume of the investment markets is at least five times greater.

In terms of its geographic and demographic spread, the securities industry outreaches most others. There are more than 4,000 registered securities firms that employ about 300,000 people, including investment advisors and financial planners. They are located in every state and are widely represented in investment markets abroad. More than 200,000 people work in the investment divisions of commercial banks, insurance companies, and other institutions whose primary sources of revenue are derived from activities other than investing.

EXAMPLES FROM A COAST-TO-COAST FLIGHT

The best overview of the securities industry in action can be obtained from a plane flying coast-to-coast or border-to-border. Follow your imagination skyward.

The plane you board, a product of one of the major aircraft manufacturers, represents a half-century or more of development effort. It embodies, too, the three kinds of resources behind all products and services—our human resources, our raw material resources, and our financial resources.

Aircraft manufacturers have a heavy reliance on all three. The company which produces your plane employs some 81,000 people who use up mountains of raw materials each year. The company also has a hefty capitalization, about $1.5 billion in all. Of this, about $1.4 billion is stockholders' equity and the remainder long-term debt. (See Glossary).

Much of the capitalization came from retained earnings, but a sizable chunk of it originated over the years through the distribution of stocks and bonds. In the sale of these issues, securities firms acted as intermediaries by first buying the issues from the aircraft manufacturer and then selling them to the investing public.

The major role of the securities industry is to act as the

middle-man in marshaling the surplus funds in the economy and make them available to finance the production of goods and services. The mechanisms for effecting these transfers are the capital markets and the money markets.

Financing by Municipal Bonds

Fasten your seat belts. Your plane is preparing to take off. As you taxi along the runway, you are traveling across an airport whose construction costs were financed by an issue of revenue bonds. These are tax-exempt securities issued by a local or state authority, although they are not obligations of the locality or state. Municipal bonds of this sort, underwritten and distributed by investment bank/brokerage firms, are frequently used, too, to finance such projects as college dormitories and urban transit systems.

As you take off, the city drops behind you. It could be any city—San Francisco or New York, Atlanta or Boston, Chicago or Houston. What all American cities have in common is an insatiable need for funds to build and maintain schools and sewers, parks and prisons, streets and avenues, or other public works by the score. Thousands and thousands of communities smaller than metropolises have similar needs, lesser in terms of dollar amounts but of equal urgency. Added to this are the financial needs of the parent state governments and state agencies.

Nationally, this means that more than one million municipal issues in circulation, or more than $20 billion in municipal bonds are brought to market each year by the securities industry.

Several kinds of transportation arteries begin to criss-cross the surface below as your plane moves along. Most prevalent are the interstate highways, a nationwide network which is engineered, organized, and largely financed by the federal government. While much of the costs were met from federal taxes on gasoline, additional billions of dollars came from the market-making efforts of an elite group of securities firms that buy and sell U.S. government issues.

Financing by Commercial Paper

Automobiles are moving to and from all points of the compass. The huge majority of them are bought on the installment plan. Finance companies lend a sizable slice of these funds, first tapping pools of capital by issuing commercial paper, i.e., corporate IOU's for repayment usually over short-term periods up to 270 days. Commercial paper, much of it sold through securities firms as dealers/middlemen, is one of the fastest growing money market instruments. Total amounts outstanding, now approaching $100 billion, have been repeatedly setting new records in recent years.

Financing by Mortgage Bonds

Those twin silver ribbons reflecting in the sun are railroad tracks, the first transportation links between east and west. There's a freight train—the steel wheel on the steel rail is still the most durable and efficient form of surface transportation around. Even from up here it's obviously a long train, over a hundred boxcars spanning a half mile. The train represents a huge investment on the move, the underlying securities being mortgage bonds and trust certificates sold to institutional investors by investment banks.

Financing by Preferred Stock

At the head of the railroad you can see a port city on one of the Great Lakes. The wake of a freighter is much more visible than the ship itself heading into port. It's a container ship, one of a fleet financed through an issue of preferred stock marketed by an investment banking syndicate. (See Glossary.)

Financing by "Pass-throughs"

Do you see that string of houses going up in the suburbs surrounding the port city? They obviously are single-family residences. Most families finance the puchase of their homes through mortgages issued by commercial banks, savings and loan associations, and other thrift institutions. When the federal government guarantees the repayment of these mortgages they are known as Fannie Maes; when they are backed by other quasi-government agencies they are known as Ginni Maes. (See Glossary).

Another enduring characteristic of Wall Street is its capacity for converting anything with a cash-flow dimension into an investable security. In recent years, mortgage bankers and other intermediaries have bundled Fannies and Ginnies into investment vehicles known as "pass-throughs". Investment banks purchase these mortgage bundles and sell them at a reasonable mark-up to institutions that invest long-term. As the principal is paid down and the interest paid up by homeowners, the cash flow thus generated is passed through by the mortgage originators to the institutions.

The houses back there in the port city suburbs, fast disappearing below the horizon, will be neither Fannie-mothered nor Ginnie-mothered. Instead, their mortgages will involve the very latest innovation in pass-throughs—Tax-exempt single-family mortgage revenue bonds issued by local governments.

These pass-throughs are so new that the investment community has yet to come up with a final designation, except that the formal title thus far has been shortened to "mortgage subsidy bonds." If these new debt instruments survive the legal tests heading their way, we can expect further acronymic recognition. Consistent with such feminine labels as Fannie and Ginnie, would Tammie Maes be appropriate? Appropriate or not, let's make tentative use of this descriptor.

Here's the why and how of Tammie Maes...

- By 1978, inflationary boosts in the price of houses and in mortgage interest rates threatened to put new single-family homes completely beyond the reach of middle-income and low-income families. These families, fully aware of the inflation-resistant advantages of real estate investments, complained to local government officials that they could not become homeowners without financial assistance.
- Local governments, including state agencies, began issuing tax-exempt revenue bonds. Investment bank syndicates bought the bonds on an interim basis with funds raised in the form of short-term commercial bank loans.
- The proceeds of the bond issues then were made available to mortgage originators for the special purpose of helping lower-income families finance the purchase of their homes. The tax-exempt feature of the bonds enabled the local governments to market them at a minimum interest cost, and this resulted in homebuyers obtaining mortgages with significantly lower interest rates than otherwise would have been the case.
- The underwriters, i.e., the investment bank syndicates, sold the revenue bonds to institutional investors and used the proceeds to pay off their commercial bank loans.
- The institutional investors got tax-exempt securities with long-term high yields.

The case history of the Tammie Maes shows how the securities industry (investment banks) relies on both the capital markets (institutional investors) and money markets (commercial banks) in functioning as a financial intermediary.

It demonstrates, too, the innovative talents of securities firms in devising new techniques to meet the public's needs. An investment bank was the advisor to the municipality that first issued Tammie Maes and was the key underwriter in marketing them. Other investment banks filled similar roles in subsequent issues for other municipalities. Advising municipalities is a long-standing investment banking service.

Home mortgages gobble up the biggest chunk of the economy's surplus funds each year. As the 1970s were ending, this amounted to about $90 billion annually and was a greater draw on the capital and money markets than the borrowings of the U.S. Government.

Securities firms, in finding long-term investors for packages of mortgages, help keep the originating institutions supplied with funds for making additional mortgage loans. This feed-back process is one reason why homeownership in the United States has become as widespread an American trait as apple pie.

Financing by Tax-advantaged Investments

Further evidence of the securities industry's inventive capability now moves into view as several oil-drilling rigs appear beneath your plane on the earth's vast spinning surface. What you're looking at is a TAI limited partnership at work. TAI is Wall Street short-hand for tax-advantaged investments, usually made by affluent individuals in the upper tax brackets. Securities firms market TAI projects which include real estate and gas development efforts as well as oil. High risk projects of this sort are encouraged by the federal government in order to add to the country's stockpile of natural resources and real assets. Individuals with income to spare can avoid passing it along to the Internal Revenue Service (IRS) by investing it in a TAI project that has a more favorable tax status. Securities firms tailor TAI projects to fit the objectives of investors as well as to generate the cash flow needed by the project operators.

Establishing Other Financial Resources

The panorama below changes from oil field to wheat field. A monstrous combine chews its way through endless acres of March durum wheat. Durum is a hardy wheat used chiefly in making macaroni and spaghetti. The scene offers several examples of the security industry's far-reaching presence.

Farm Credit. The Federal Farm Credit Bank (FFCB) provides financial support for U.S. farmers. About $1 billion is loaned each month to agricultural producers who need funds to finance their planting, cultivating, and harvesting costs, and for other purposes during the off-market season. The farm community repays these loans after marketing its output. The original funds for these loans are derived from periodic issues of FFCB bonds that are underwritten and sold to investors by securities firms.

Farm Equipment. In the current century, farming in the United States changed dramatically from a large number of labor-intensive small producers to a comparatively small number of capital-intensive large producers. The combine you see below the plane is almost a complete factory on wheels. It carries the nameplate of one of the big farm machinery manufacturers. It also carries, when new, one of the biggest price tickets on any piece of equipment this side of Cape Kennedy. The capital structure of the manufacturer is built on some 30 million common shares, 500,000 preferred shares (which together have a market value totaling over $1 billion), plus almost $1 billion of debt issues. Over the years, investment bank syndicates have underwritten these securities and broker/dealer syndicates have sold them.

Commodities. Wheat is a commodity. A commodity is an article of trade or commerce that can be transported, especially an agricultural or mining product. Corn, apples, potatoes, hogs, chickens, turkeys, and numerous other basic foodstuffs are all commodities. There also are non-food commodities that include varieties of wood, metals, and other primary raw materials. Specialists in securities firms trade some fifty separate commodities on twelve U.S. commodity exchanges.

Trading of commodities is conducted either in the spot market or in the forward futures market. In the spot market, commodities are bought or sold for cash. In the forward market, purchases and sales of the commodities are arranged for subsequent delivery. These deliveries actually take place, in contrast to the futures market. In the futures market, contracts are traded for delivering commodities at specified dates thereafter.

The chief objective of commodity futures is hedging—i.e., insulating agricultural products and raw materials against unfavorable price fluctuations during the interim period when these commodities are inventoried and when they are marketed as finished goods. For example, a bread manufacturer has to buy wheat considerably in advance of the time for delivering sliced white. Should the price of wheat decline sharply after the manufacturer has inventoried it, it could mean substantial financial loss. The bread company offsets this possibility by selling commodity futures equal in value to the wheat inventory when purchased.

Hedging is an essential bridge for spanning the interval between wheat in the ground and bread in the toaster. In fact, the most pervasive and most indispensable of all industries, the food industry, could not function satisfactorily without the assistance of security traders specializing in commodity futures.

Similarly, the whole chain connecting agricultural production and food consumption could not have been established, nor would it hold together for very long, without the support of the securities industry. The food industry chain includes such links as farms and ranches, grain elevators and warehouses, truckers and shippers, processing and packaging, and marketing and banking. (Note: More checks are cashed in supermarkets than any place else—including the commercial banks.)

Each of the above links is a major industry. Each industry is represented in the investment markets by hundreds of millions of shares of common stock, by thousands of fixed-income securities, and by preferred stock and convertible debt issues in the hundreds. This is only the food production/distribution/consumption chain. Even though the food chain is the most important and the largest, it still is just one of many chains that bind together a gross national product (See Glossary.) in excess of $3 trillion in goods and services.

As the sun declines, dusk begins to overtake your plane. Below, the lights begin to show. Another chain becomes visible: the electric utilities—prime users of the investment markets.

For the great majority of Americans, the securities industry is like the sky—omnipresent but largely ignored. Nevertheless it is there, everywhere you look, whether you see it or not.

The captain turns on the warning sign. You fasten your seat belt. The plane coasts down an invisible slope, completes its approach, and rolls to a halt on the runway.

Overleaf: Since its emergence in the early nineteenth century, Wall Street (a symbol of New York's financial district) has been recognized as the center of the world's capital markets.

CHAPTER 2

WALL STREET: PLENTY OF PARADOXES

The symbolic capital of the securities industry traditionally has been a place where paradoxes abound.

Wall Street originally took shape as a picket fence to keep the hogs from nearby farms out of the grassy meadows and shady lanes surrounding Battery Park.

Wall Street, one of the most famous streets in the world, also is one of the shortest. You can walk its full length from Trinity Church to the East River in ten minutes. For the many millions of Americans and the thousands of investors overseas who have a direct stake in the world's greatest securities industry, however, Wall Street is the nation's longest street. It extends into each of the fifty states in its all-pervasive influence. What happens to tourisim in Hawaii, to oil production in Texas or Alaska, to the automotive industry in Michigan, or to the tobacco crop in Virginia—quickly becomes manifest in price fluctuations of representative securities. Similarly, what happens in Wall Street often sends high voltage shocks into every corner of the nation.

Like a German castle dominating the Rhine, the New York Stock Exchange historically has dominated the securities industry. For more than a century and a half, the Big Board, another name for it, appeared to be an entrenched fortress insulated from the thrusts of competitive forces. The old Wall Street, until little more than a decade ago, had pretty much conducted its basic business in the same way as when the nation was in its infancy. The securities industry had generated most of its revenues by issuing, marketing, and trading stocks and bonds. From the eighteenth century onward, the players changed, but the game didn't.

SMALL BEGINNINGS

The securities industry had its beginnings like the nation itself—struggling for freedom to determine its own fate, but small and primitive compared to larger and more strongly structured socio-economic institutions across the Atlantic.

The first formal organization of the New York markets occurred when the "buttonwood" brokers (so-named after a huge sycamore tree, also called the buttonwood tree, whose pods resembled the wooden buttons worn in those times, and in which shade they traded) signed an agreement ratifying their existence as a special interest guild. At the time, securities trading was subordinate to their primary commercial interests in banking, insurance, and factoring (lending).

The agreement signed at Corre's hotel on May 17, 1792, was the Buttonwood Tree Agreement. One day the seeds planted there would become the largest and most influential securities industry in the world. The agreement read, in part:

> "We, the subscribers, brokers for the purchase and sale of public stocks, do hereby solemnly promise and pledge ourselves to each other that we will not buy or sell from this date, for any person whatsoever, any kind of public stocks at a less rate than one-quarter of one per cent commission on the specie value, and that we will give preference to each other in our negotiations."

This was the first blueprint that prescribed the operational structure of the New York Stock Exchange. The Exchange itself did not come into existence until 1817 when representatives of seven securities firms organized it as the New York Stock and Exchange Board (subsequently to be known as the Big Board). Supplemented by the Great Charter of the New York Stock Exchange, it eventually centralized control of the securities markets among the founding brokers.

UNIQUE CONTRIBUTIONS

That there were structural flaws in the New York Stock Exchange, as well as fundamental weaknesses in its method of operation, has been demonstrated from time to time in its colorful history. This should not belittle the immense contributions of the Exchange to the development of efficient capital markets when they were needed most—in the recurring eras of accelerated economic growth. It was the New York Stock Exchange that screened applicant companies to make sure counterfeit securities would not be foisted on the investing public. It was the Exchange, too, that carefully screened securities firms, and their principals, before granting them membership.

The New York Stock Exchange, in other words, created and enforced a value system that bred confidence in individual investors that they would get a fair chance in the capital markets. Without such public faith behind it, the securities industry could not have been so favorably positioned to ride the crest of the recurring tidal waves of economic growth that bore America to the forefront of the industralized nations.

RIDING THE CREST

The first major wave was the Industrial Revolution. England was its cradle. In the latter half of the eighteenth century, steam power was first used in England to activate machinery, and for the first time a sizable body of men and a line of machines were brought together under one factory roof. Previously, in England as elsewhere, human labor and natural resources were the elements of survival. People tilled small patches of soil for sustenance, or they worked individually with their own hands in manufacturing articles in their own homes or shops. Their horizons seldom extended beyond eyesight range. For the most part, the communities where they were born were the communities where they lived and died.

By the 1760s, much of the textile production in England was mechanized. Before the eighteenth century ended, there were forty times as many people with jobs in the textile industry—and all of them getting higher wages for shorter working hours.

The advent of the industrial era vastly expanded the dimensions of human life. It also created a new economic need to sustain humanity's progress thereafter: the need for capital resources. In the industrial world, capital resources would become as essential to economic growth as human and natural resources.

The industrial revolution in America did not build up momentum until the latter half of the nineteenth century. But once it got rolling, its progress was incredible!

One reason was that never before in the history of civilization had there been such an ideal combination of human resources, natural resources, and financial resources available to so many people eager to use them. Hundreds of thousands of immigrants had expanded the work force significantly; as the nation unrolled to the west, abundant raw materials were discovered across the land; the invention of the telegraph in 1844, the ticker system in 1867, and telephones in 1878 enabled the securities industry to extend its reach from coast-to-coast.

THE INDUSTRY COMES OF AGE

The Civil War was the catalyst that solidified the loosely-connected securities firms in the various thriving cities of the North into a single industry. Salmon P. Chase, President Lincoln's Secretary of the Treasury, was faced with the huge task of raising some $500 million to cover the Union's costs of waging the war. To direct this effort, he turned to his brother-in-law, Jay Cooke.

Cooke, a Wall Street financier of some prominence, also was the sort of financial entrepreneur who couldn't resist the challenge of breaking new ground. He agreed to marshal the human forces that would be needed to raise $500 million, "an inconceivably large sum of money at that time," as one historian has described it.

It was obvious to Cooke that no one securities firm could even begin to round up the funds. His solution was to organize the first selling syndicate. It included some of the more prominent securities firms in New York, as well as those in Baltimore and Boston.

The issue of bonds had a 6 percent coupon. To sell them to private investors, Cooke and the other members of the syndicate organized a sales force of 2,500 who literally blanketed every city, town, and village in the North. A hard-hitting, far-reaching advertising campaign supported the sales force in the field. The bonds were well received throughout the Union and European investors also bought a sizable portion of the issue.

STEADY GROWTH FOR DECADES—ALMOST

The nation's explosive economic growth was resumed after the tragic conflict. Before the war, there had been three millionaires in the United States. In 1900, there were about 4,000. (In 1978, there were 520,000). The growth statistics of the nation's mighty economic advance on the wave of the industrial revolution make memorable reading. For example, in 1849 there were 957,000 wage earners whose products were valued at slightly more than $1 billion. In 1929, there were 8.8 million wage earners turning out products valued at more than $70 billion.

The securities markets grew rapidly and in step with commercial and industrial development. Not only did their dimensions increase but also their numbers. By 1868, there were four sizable trading centers in vigorous competition with the New York Stock Exchange: the Open Board, the Petroleum and Mining Board, the Gold Exchange, and at the south end of Broad Street, the Curb. Some idea of how far the securities markets had come in New York from their simple beginnings under the buttonwood tree can be seen in some of the trading volume figures for 1868. About $3 billion of securities were sold at the New York Stock Exchange, with even larger volumes being handled by the Open Board and impressive volumes by the Curb brokers.

The continuing increase in the volume and variety of shares traded on these markets affirmed New York City's stature as the unquestionable financial capital of the nation. After the Open Board was merged into the New York Stock Exchange, from 1869 onward the New York Exchange was the dominant institution, without challenge, on Wall Street.

The growth of the securities markets in the latter half of the nineteenth century was not upward in a straight line. As a tail on a kite, the boom-and-bust cycles of the economy resulted in wild soaring and swooping of stock prices. The real test of the resilience of the securities markets came in the six years of depression that followed the 1873 panic.

The depression and the attendant bear market (see Glossary) were the longest in the nation's history up to that time. Over 280 brokerage firms declared bankruptcy. The price of a seat on the

Big Board in 1876 was $4,000, down from almost $8,000 before the depression. But the securities markets survived and flourished in the recovery that got underway in 1879.

The development of the early securities firms closely paralleled the development of the U.S. economy. Before the tidal wave of the industrial revolution rolled in from Europe in the latter half of the nineteenth century, government bodies were small. The great majority of communities were rurally oriented since the nation essentially was an agricultural economy consisting of small family-run farms. Commercial and business enterprises for the most part were modest one-family operations. The development of canals and the push of the railroads, plus the infusion of considerable capital from European investors, greatly accelerated the expansion of the securities industry as the nineteenth century progressed.

Still, for the most part, typical securities firms were small businesses. Many of them were organized as bases of operations for the investment tycoons whose speculative and manipulative activities were rarely reported in the press, except when the Vanderbilts, Fisks, Drews and Goulds made newspaper headlines in the course of making—and losing—overnight fortunes. The deception of the plungers and manipulators contributed nothing to the investment markets except unfavorable publicity. The securities industry laid a durable foundation in the nineteenth century in spite of, rather than as a result of, the unbridled speculations and embezzlements of manipulators.

By the turn of the century, the New York Stock Exchange had become nationwide in scope. Its member firms had branch offices in all major cities, and regional securities houses maintained correspondent relationships with Big Board members. Besides traditional broker/dealer trading services, investment banking services also were becoming an essential part of the securities industry as the new century dawned.

The House of Morgan already had become the most respected—and feared—investment bank in the nation. Under the strong hand of J.P. Morgan, the firm added to its renown as "the Doctor of Wall Street," a nickname reflecting its success in reorganizing the railroads and eliminating their throat-cutting rate competition. Morgan's success in reorganizing and consolidating industrial corporations, as well as railroads, was shared by such important houses as Kuhn Loeb, Harris Forbes, and Speyer & Co.

This signified the opening of a new frontier for the fraternity—and it was at least that—of the big investment banks. Their influence as financial advisors and investment bankers took on a potent new dimension. They became directors as well as underwriters (see Glossary) for most of the blue-chip industrial corporations. Their peripheral function as investment/financial advisors thus became internalized as corporate decision-makers.

The marriage of investment banking to industry was to continue as an intimate relationship for three quarters of a century. Only in recent years have these ties been loosened by shifting economic pressures.

EFFECTS OF WORLD WAR I

With the outbreak of World War I, the London Stock Exchange shut down as the city concentrated its activities in support of Britain's war effort. The war precipitated a selling wave that swept into Wall Street from all financial centers abroad. Overwhelmed with selling orders, the Big Board responded by firmly closing its doors. The Exchange, in effect, was out to lunch from July 31, 1914, until mid-December. In November, trading on the New York Curb Market (renamed the American Stock Exchange in 1953) began to show renewed signs of life. This prompted the Big Board governors to get back in business the following month.

During the years of neutrality, U.S. industry received an immense stimulus from the Allies' war needs. In 1914, about 45 million long tons of iron ore were mined; by 1917 this had increased to 71 million. During the war, including the period after America's entry, U.S. production of coal tar chemicals grew tenfold. The market value of drugs produced rose from $177 million annually to $418 million.

The securities industry, its fate and fortunes rooted in the economy, also expanded geometrically. Patterned after the Jay Cooke prototype, Liberty Loan drives expanded and intensified the interest of millions of Americans in securities as a savings reservoir and source of income.

The first World War resulted in three major changes for the United States:

- The U.S. economy was transformed into the most powerful in the world.
- New York superseded London as the world's financial capital.
- The stage was set for the most speculative decade in the history of the United States—in fact, in the history of any nation since the tulip mania in the seventeenth century. (The market value of a single tulip bulb in European trading centers was equal to $10,000.)

ROARING TO DISASTER

The Roaring Twenties actually started in low gear. The postwar bull market ran into a stone wall in July 1920, when stock prices declined by more than 30 percent. Although the pro-business Republican Party won a landslide for Warren Harding in the presidential election, it did not put a platform under the crumbling stock market as some forecasters had predicted. Instead, between election day and Christmas, stock prices dropped by more than 20 percent.

After two years of stagnation, the economy began to recover in the summer of 1921 with a big assist from the Federal Reserve System, which lived up to its name by pumping reserves into the business and consumer sectors through the commercial banks. Eight years of almost uninterrupted economic growth followed with virtually no inflation. It was the longest period of sustained prosperity on record, with industrial production up by almost 100% and the gross national product showing a 50% advance.

Securities prices and trading volume were to rise even faster. The Dow Jones average of leading stocks, for example, quadrupled in the 1921-1929 span. Millions of Americans, their interest in the securities markets spurred by the Liberty Loan drives and their purses fat with war-savings, became get-rich-quick speculators.

The big commercial banks were in the thick of it, not only as speculators for their own portfolios, but also—and more devastatingly—as the most lavish lenders in financial history. From the end of 1924 to the end of 1928, bank securities loans tripled, rising from about $2 billion to $6 billion. Big industrial lenders also were shooting call money into Wall Street. Their loans during the same period increased even faster, from $550 million to almost $4 billion.

More and more people were "in the market." A list of utility preferred stockholders published in 1928 virtually was a cross-section of businessmen, craftsmen, and just plain people. Heading the list were housekeepers (4,029), clerks (2,987), factory workers (1,058), as well as bankers and brokers, barbers and bricklayers, and 50 categories in between. Now almost everyone was "in the market."

Borrow money. Buy stocks. Watch the prices go up.

Borrow more money. Buy more stocks—continue borrowing on smaller margins. Extend your risk yet more.

It could end only one way—disaster and collapse.

The great collapse of the securities markets in 1929, and the great depression that followed, have become well-known landmarks of U.S. economic history.

Overleaf: The volume of trading in the 1960s grew faster than ever before. (John Maguire, Matar Studio, Inc.)

CHAPTER 3

WALL STREET: BETWEEN THE ACTS

The securities industry was battered as much as any other sector during the 1930s. Even so, it benefited from much needed reforms. The extent of public participation in the securities markets clearly had demonstrated in the 1920s that Wall Street's business was the public's business as well. Resentment against the commercial banks and securities firms, which had foisted counterfeit securities on a gullible public, was nationwide. Congress heard loud and clear the clamor for reform.

The result was the Securities Act of 1933, and the Securities Exchange Act of 1934. The 1933 Act established regulations that ordered full disclosure of all pertinent information about new security issues before their distribution to the investing public. The 1934 Act imposed regulatory control on the trading markets and created the Securities and Exchange Commission (the SEC) to assure that the markets would function "freely and fairly in the public interest."

Will Rogers, the first standup comic to wear a sombrero, put it most succinctly: "Congress has put a cop on the corner of Wall Street."

Leaders of the securities industry had fought the reform measures as hard as they could—in Congress, in the press, and by enlisting the support of influential businessmen.

"If this legislation is passed," they warned, "grass will grow on Wall Street." Forty years later, they would make the same protest when the Reform Act of 1975 was under consideration.

What grew instead was a much stronger securities industry. While the SEC did function as a cop on the corner of Wall Street, to all intents and purposes the New York Stock Exchange remained the self-regulated dominant institution of the securities industry. The Big Board retained control of its price-fixing privileges, insulated from meaningful competition.

Still, if the Securities Acts of the thirties did not make the securities markets completely free and fair, they did make them free enough and fair enough to restore and sustain the confidence of the investing public in time for the great period of economic growth that followed World War II.

AN ERA OF PROFOUND CHANGE IN THE INDUSTRY

Anyone familiar with the securities industry in the early 1950's would agree that it has become a totally new industry. These changes have been as widespread as they have been profound. The period following World War II and lasting until the end of the 1960s was one of the most remarkable periods of sustained economic growth in the history of the United States—or of any other country. Fundamental changes in the overall economy could only imply derivative changes in the securities industry.

Conditions Triggering Change

A unique combination of factors stimulated U.S. economic expansion after World War II:

- Externally, there were the immense reconstruction needs of the war-decimated economies of Europe and Asia. Among all the industrialized nations participating in the war, only America's productive capacity emerged intact.

- Internally, war-related shortages of goods and services had created massive demands at all income levels and in all geographic sectors of the United States.
- Politically, the Marshall Plan and other programs helped Europe and Japan struggle to their feet and provided them with the financial assistance to import from the United States the vast supply of capital and consumer goods they needed.
- Financially, Americans had built up an unprecedented store of purchasing power through investments in savings bonds and other liquid assets. The commercial banking system was awash with liquidity in the form of swollen inventories of U.S. government securities.
- A broad array of new synthetic materials (fibers, plastics, synthetic rubber, drugs, etc.) were created in the war years to supplement America's natural resources. New industries appeared on all sides.
- An ample supply of labor was on hand as millions of armed forces personnel discarded their uniforms.

There it was: the ideal combination of human resources, natural resources, and financial resources. Stimulated by unprecedented worldwide demand for all kinds of industrial and consumer products and services, by the time the 1950s had begun, the American economy had completed its war-to-peace transition and was surging ahead in high gear.

Remarkably, aside from a relatively short burst of inflationary pressures associated with the Korean conflict, American economic expansion was relatively inflation-free until the late 1960s. Like a starving crocodile, once inflation would begin to chew on the U.S. economy, its appetite would be insatiable.

Inevitable Growth of the Securities Industry

The securities industry, in keeping with Wall Street's predilection for the paradoxical, experienced two separate and seemingly contradictory kinds of growth during the great expansion era of the 1950s-1970s. For the most part, the investment community expanded in all directions in the 50s and 60s; but in the 70s some sectors of the securities markets and their participants began to contract. Yet for the 1950-1975 quarter century as a whole, the overall growth of the securities industry in general matched that of the entire economy.

The industry's growth in the 1950s, to a major degree, reflected the increased participation in the securities market of individual investors. The massive rise in the economy lifted the standard of living of the average American family well above all previous waterlines. Unprecedented and sustained boosts in real discretionary income left consumers with surplus funds. As happened to their forefathers four generations earlier, investing in securities during a great war conditioned Americans to putting some savings in stocks and bonds in peacetime. The greatest flow of funds directly from individuals went into stocks or into mutual funds whose assets consisted chiefly of common shares. The number of individuals owning shares of stock or shares of mutual funds increased fivefold in the 1950s and 1960s. By 1970, over 30 million individual stockholders owned some 40 billion shares of stock with a total market value well in excess of $1 trillion.

The rising affluence of Mr. and Mrs. America in the golden era of the 1950s and 1960s resulted, too, in a continuous flow of billions of dollars from residual personal income into the funds of institutional investors. These included, besides mutual funds whose sole purpose was investing, life insurance companies, savings banks, pension funds, retirement funds, profit sharing plans, combined trusts administered by bank trust departments, common trusts, investment clubs, and several other varieties of institutional intermediaries.

As the institutions received an increasing flow of funds, their role as influential forces in the securities markets increased accordingly. By 1961, the several kinds of insurance companies and bank trust departments, together with foundations and college endowment funds, owned a total of more than $30 billion in listed stocks alone. Mutual funds held an additional $17 billion, noninsured pension funds almost $18 billion, and closed-end trusts about $6 billion.

The increased institutionalization of the securities markets in the 1950s and 1960s resulted in the investment community attaching one of its characteristic short names to institutional investors—i.e., the "buy side." The "sell side" of course referred to Wall Street firms which were, for the most part, members of the New York Stock Exchange or other exchanges, and active participants in the over-the-counter markets.

The sell side of the Street in the early fifties could be divided into two categories, the brokerage houses and the investment banks. As the decade began, there was a clear-cut delineation between the brokerage houses buying and selling securities for their customers on the one hand, and the investment banks chiefly involved on the other hand in generating new issues of securities for their corporate or governmental customers.

New Emphasis on Training and Marketing

As the fifties ended, the list of the ten largest firms in each category showed an emerging giant astride both camps, Merrill Lynch, Pierce, Fenner & Smith. It was the one securities firm that did the most to unite Wall Street to Main Street, and the one firm above all others that had its finger on the growth pulse of the securities industry. As the 1950s ended, Merrill Lynch had over 500,000 customers and its brokerage revenues were larger than the combined totals of its next four largest brokerage competitors.

What was the secret of Charles Merrill's success? Merrill, essentially, was a marketing man—in fact, a mass marketing man with considerable experience with such large retail chains as Kresge, Safeway, and McCrory. Merrill also had spent some time with several Wall Street firms, beginning in the clerical ranks but gradually working up the ladder to more responsible and rewarding roles selling bonds and managing offerings.

After he started his own firm, he had two assets: he knew how important confidence was as a determinant of why people spent their money and put their savings in one place rather than another; and he knew that there was an enormous reservoir of savings in the hands of middle-income America.

What was the secret of his success? Robert Sobel, in "The Big Board", has put it as succinctly as anyone else:

> "The secrets of Charles Merrill's success were amazingly simple and so obvious that by the mid-1950s almost every brokerage in the (financial) district had adopted some of them. Merrill instituted rigorous training programs for his salesmen, who, during the firm's earlier days, were paid straight salaries and no commissions. He then made sure his customers were apprised of their broker's training and remuneration. In the past, Wall Street had been plagued by incompetents whose major interest was switching customers in and out of stocks in order to make higher commissions. Because of this, many customers (who remembered the twenties and early thirties) mistrusted the entire financial community. Merrill set out to reverse this feeling, and to a large extent, succeeded."

Essentially, the boom in the securities markets in the 1950s and 1960s reflected the public's interest in equity issues. Although there was the recurring cyclical recessions and recoveries, interest rates remained within unexciting boundaries. The action in the capital markets centered on stocks and convertibles; straight fixed-income was for the "prudent men," the institutional buyers.

The institutions, the "buy" side, had a legally-trusted responsibility in the 1960s to conserve, as well as enhance, the assets entrusted to them. Such big organizational money managers as the insurance companies and bank trust departments traditionally had regarded capital preservation as the top priority in investing hundreds of billions of dollars in behalf of their corporate and individual customers. It was common practice to invest the great bulk of these funds in top-rated bonds with a much smaller part channeled into a "legal list" of equities. The legal list consisted of a select group of securities approved by state regulatory authorities for trust investment. A commonplace target of big organizational money managers was about 80 percent in debt issues, ten to 15 percent in equities, and the remainder in cash. This had been their overall investment policy, that is, before "the dynamic fifties and swinging sixties."

New Developments Bring Further Change

Several developments, which materialized in these fat years, had dramatic impact on the customary buy-it-and-put-it-away policies of the large institutional investors:

The Success of Organized Labor in Obtaining Increased Pension and Profit-Sharing Benefits from Business and Industrial Employers. This vastly expanded the cash-flow actuarial requirements of pension and profit-sharing plans and put new emphasis on the importance of capital appreciation in money management.

Emergence of a New Generation of "Performance-Oriented" Money Managers. They had a number of characteristics in common: they were comparatively young; they had no experience with the sort of fierce bear market that an earlier generation of money managers had to contend with in the 1930s; they scoffed at capital preservation as an investment management policy and glorified the concept of capital gains; and they were not at all reticent about having their money management techniques exploited by sensation-seeking publications ("Can the Bond Market Survive?").

The Swift Growth of Mutual Funds. From a pre-World War II base of less than $15 billion, the asset value of these investment companies tripled in the post-war boom years. Although the "performance" funds actually represented only a very small slice of the assets managed by all institutional investors, including the more conservative mutual funds, still the "go-go" funds (as they were known in Wall Street slang) were in the limelight and helped attract hundreds of thousands of new purchasers of mutual fund shares.

Escalation of Price/Earnings Multiples. The intensified interest in stocks raised the price-earnings multiples of corporations to record levels. This triggered an unprecedented wave of corporate mergers. Hundreds of high p/e companies, led by the conglomerates, acquired the equities of lower p/e companies. (In effect, a company with a p/e of 14 could use $1 of its earnings to buy $2 of earnings of a company whose p/e was 7.)

Attractiveness of New Issues. New issues based on high p/e ratios became a very attractive method of raising corporate capital. In 1969, for example, new issues of common and preferred stock totaled $9.3 billion, up by more than a third from the previous year.

The new issue syndrome soon became the favorite toy of individual investors. As one financial publication described it:

> "The public's mania for new issues almost was unbelievable. Since almost any new issue early in 1961 could be expected to show a price jump of as much as thirty or forty percent during the first trading day, there was an insane scramble among individual investors to get in on any new offering that came along."

The merger wave also rolled over Wall Street. As the volume of trading expanded, the overhead and other operational costs of securities firms rose accordingly. A severe market break occurred in 1962. Coming on the heels of a substantial increase in trading volume in 1961, it trapped many investment firms between first and second base. A significant number of firms, whose business was concentrated in over-the-counter stocks, went bankrupt. Big Board member firms generally were spared this fate. However, consolidations among these firms took place right and left. Over fifty mergers were consummated in 1963.

WEAKNESSES LEADING TO THE SECOND ACT

The volume of trading in the sixties grew even faster than during the hectic fifties—thanks to "go-go gunslingers."

In fact, trading expanded so fast that it brought Wall Street to its knees. The volume of unfulfilled transactions in 1967-68 introduced the investing public to a new bit of jargon: "fails," from the failure of securities firms and the exchanges to consummate trading transactions.

The volume of trading reached avalanche proportions in 1968. Almost 3.3 billion shares were traded on the New York Exchange that year, up by 130% from the total volume in 1964; and there was a gain of over 170% on the American Exchange during the same period.

The Big Board responded to this explosive increase in its business by reducing its trading hours. By the end of 1968 the fails crunch had affected $4 billion of market transactions—$4 billion in securities whose precise whereabouts were unknown. Public criticism was widespread and severe. Congress voiced innumerable misgivings and undertook several investigations. There were repeated statements of "concern" by the SEC.

It was obvious as the sixties drew to a close that there was something fundamentally wrong with the investment markets— obvious, particularly, to congressional committees involved with the industry. A marketplace basically is a turntable where merchandise comes in from sellers and is delivered to buyers. When the turntable doesn't work, when it "fails" to pick up and deliver the goods, the confidence of buyers and sellers is bound to decrease.

There were several fundamental weaknesses that caused the breakdown of the investment turntable in the latter years of the sixties. For example:

- The "gunslingers" had chased the sheriffs and federal marshalls out of town. Said the "go-go" gang: "It's pure garble that the law and order forces of capital preservation should be the overriding guidelines of investing; it's nonsense that diversification of risk minimizes potential loss; it's smart to concentrate on a few issues in order to cut down on comissions and overhead at the same time. With law and order absent up in the hills, let's have a whack, everyone, at the gambling table. Volume—overnight get-rich-quick volume—but volume there must be," they said.
- All other industries, other than the securities industry, had invested many billions of dollars, hundreds of billions, perhaps, in information-transfer technology in the post-World War II decades—in electronic data processing, in automatic order routing and order transactions, in computer-controlled information retrieval systems, and in telecommunications. In comparison, the securities industry had an information transfer capability that was only several steps removed from the pony express.
- Business relationships in the investment markets were insulated from the sharpening frictions of the grindstones of competition. In the business world at large, as on the racetrack, it really isn't money that makes the horse move: it's competition. Money is the reward that the horse gets after successful performance in the public markets. It's competition that spurs the horse to perform effectively. In the investment markets, services were neither bought nor sold on a strictly competitive basis. Frank, the senior portfolio decision-maker at the Gargantua Bank & Trust Company, bought security trading services from Whippet & Greyhound because Harry, senior partner at the Wall

Street firm, was an old friend. And Harry knew all about give-ups; in fact, Bert over at Turtle, Bayside & Kismet, the research boutique, was an old friend of both Frank and Harry.

Is this an exaggeration of the way business was conducted in the old securities industry? A slight exaggeration, perhaps, since not all the business of the old industry consisted of the left hand washing the right hand with both hands washing the wrists. The point is that the old securities industry, after two centuries of only minor evolutionary changes, has been significantly transformed by the revolutionary changes of the seventies: The Reform Act of 1975, ERISA[1], growing inflation, and unprecedentedly high interest rates. Historically, the new securities industry has set sail for unexplored shores. Change is the watchword. Change, the double-barreled synonym: problems for those imprisoned in the past; or opportunities for those free to make the most of the present and future.

---

[1] The Employee Retirement Income Security Act of 1974. See pages 46–49.

Overleaf: The buyers of securities include corporations, governments and institutions, as well as individuals. All of these employ the most astute analysts and managers of their investment funds.

CHAPTER 4

THE BUY SIDE OF THE WHOLESALE MARKET

Some anonymous wise man was credited with saying that the safest way of explaining something complicated is to pretend that it is simple, and that the safest way of explaining something simple is to pretend that it is complicated. What does this mean? Was this a complicated wise man pretending to be simple, or a simple wise man pretending to be complicated?

The best way to explain how the securities business functions is to keep it simple, realizing that, like any other business, it functions in a marketplace. The merchandise the securities business brings to the marketplace consists of investment services. As in all markets, there are buyers and sellers.

More precisely, the securities business merchandises its services in two markets, a wholesale market and a retail market. There are four kinds of buyers in the wholesale market:

- Corporations: includes companies and other business entities
- Federal government bodies: includes government agencies and international bodies
- Local governments: includes states, state agencies and municipalities
- Institutional investors: includes bank trust departments, insurance companies, pension and endowment funds, investment companies, etc.

Each of these entities will be discussed in order.

CORPORATIONS AS BUYERS OF SERVICES

Corporations buy a considerable variety of investment services in the wholesale market. The most important item on their shopping list is the use of capital. The key word in that sentence is "use." The security industry does not, except in special circumstances, put out its own capital to hire. Instead, as indicated earlier, it acts chiefly as a middle-man, or agent, in arranging access for corporate users to surplus funds. In this case, the securities industry functions somewhat like a marriage broker.

The corporate buyer obtains the use of capital either in the form of equity or as debt. More often than not, the buyer pays for equity capital by issuing shares (common or preferred stock) and paying dividends on the ownership rights which these certificates represent to the shareholders.

The use of debt is obtained by the corporate buyer through issuing bonds, notes, or other types of securities that investors get as a claim on the issuer's assets and earning power. Debt issues, as a rule, do not represent ownership rights. Investors are paid for the use of their funds in the form of interest during the life of the securities and are repaid their initial investments in the debt securities when they mature.

Private placements increasingly have become a favorite method whereby corporate buyers of the use of funds have tapped the capital markets. A private placement allows the corporate user to bypass the time-consuming and tedious requirements of offering an issue in the open market. A securities firm, the usual go-between, lines up a big institutional investor such as an insurance company (or a group of investors) and the corporate user thereby can place the issue of securities directly in the investors' hands. The securities firm gets a fee for its services.

Private placement growth has been impressive in the sixties and seventies. Of the total gross corporate offerings of stocks and bonds amounting to $45 billion to $50 billion annually, over half in recent years has been in the form of private placements.

The natural question would be: why don't all corporate users go the private placement route? There are several answers: it costs more for the corporate user (in terms of interest rates) to make a private placement; a private placement usually requires a firm commitment on the part of the borrower to pay the stipulated interest rate over the life of the issue with no recourse to advance refunding; and closely regulated industries, such as the public utilities, are prevented from making private placements for a number of reasons. Since the utilities tap the capital markets each year for as much as $18 to $20 billion, the open market will remain an indispensable mechanism for raising utility capital as well as capital needed by other sectors of the economy.

THE FEDERAL GOVERNMENT AS BUYER OF SERVICES

Uncle Sam, while not the biggest buyer of capital use, certainly is the most influential. The rates accorded U.S. government debt issues have a powerful effect upon rates throughout the capital and money markets.

Treasury bills, the most prevalent form of U.S. issues, normally have a life span of ninety-one days, at which time the funds raised by the bills are displaced by new issues of bills. Treasury bills do not bear interest coupons but instead are sold at a discount from their face value. Investors thereby get paid for the use of their funds when the T-bills are retired at full face value at maturity.

Treasury bills also are issued in longer maturities than ninety-one days—for six-month, nine-month, and one-year maturities as well. The minimum purchase of each bill is for $10,000. Treasury bills are favored investment vehicles for the whole spectrum of investors. For example, an analysis of a total of T-bills outstanding recently showed that of the aggregate of approximately $80 billion, 40 percent were held by Federal Reserve Banks and U.S. government accounts; 25 percent by commercial banks, insurance companies, and other large institutions; 15 percent by foreign investors; 8 percent by state and local governments; 8 percent by individuals; and the remainder by corporations and miscellaneous groups.

Another type of security issued by Uncle Sam that competes with a T-bill is the certificate of indebtedness. This differs from a T-bill in that it does bear an interest coupon, but like a T-bill, its maturity does not exceed one year.

Tax anticipation bills are generally of the same genre as T-bills and certificates of indebtedness, except that they are issued irregularly. There may be from one to six issues each year, timed to increase the stability of cash flow from tax payments into the Treasury. Their advantage to the investor is that they usually mature a week after an income tax payment date and can be used at face value in payment of taxes. In addition, the investor receives a bonus of a week's interest. These securities are of particular interest to corporate taxpayers who must set aside part of their income as a reserve against future tax payments.

Treasury notes and treasury bonds, whose maturities normally extend from one year to as many as twenty years, are two major types of Uncle Sam's securities that have interest coupons. The notes, which are normally issued to mature in not less than one year nor more than seven, usually are bearer form only—meaning that they are highly negotiable and can be traded readily without the usual intermediary steps that registered bonds require. The minimum denomination for the purchase of notes is $1,000.

Treasury bonds usually have longer maturities than notes, as well as a ceiling on the amount of interest that can be paid on them—a ceiling which, having been established by Congress, has been recurringly adjusted upward since World War II. The minimum denomination for investing in a government bond is $1,000, aside from Savings Bonds (Series E) that can be purchased for $50 and multiples thereof.

Until a few years ago, there were a half dozen or so federal agencies issuing securities in the wholesale market for a variety of uses, mainly to provide funds in support of the housing and agricultural sectors of the economy. The agricultural agencies affected have been lumped together under a single umbrella, the Federal Farm Credit Bank, which buys the use of funds in the wholesale markets, in place of the former Banks for Cooperatives, the Federal Intermediate Credit Banks, and the Federal Land Banks.

Although these interest-coupon securities, including those of the housing agencies, are not officially guaranteed by the federal government (the issuing agency is the guarantor), most institutional investors regard this as a distinction without much of a difference. In their view, since the agencies are federal government chartered, Uncle Sam still stands behind the agency securities—even though one step removed.

These agency securities have been gradually enlarging their share of the capital markets. As much as $50 billion can be outstanding in a given year. One overriding reason for their popularity in the institutional investor market is that there is no ceiling on their coupon rates, as in the case of U.S. bonds. Usually their coupons offer an inviting differential to long-term investors.

Aside from Uncle Sam and other national governments that buy the use of funds in American capital markets, a number of international and supranational agencies also purchase this investment service. They include such financing bodies as the Inter-American Development Bank, the European Investment Bank, the European Coal & Steam Community, and many others. Their aggregate borrowings exceed $100 billion.

MUNICIPAL GOVERNMENT AS A BUYER OF SERVICES

In a sense, the term "municipal" is a blanket bit of terminology. It covers not only securities issued by states and their subcommunities (cities, towns, regional bodies, etc.), but also those issued by territories and possessions of the United States and their political subdivisions, or by authorities or commissions.

Municipal securities most frequently take the form of bonds, ordinarily issued in denominations of $1,000 or $5,000. Investors often have the option of obtaining them as bearer (fully negotiable bonds like cash), or as registered instruments. Almost invariably, municipal bonds have interest payments on a six-month basis; and the common practice is simply to clip the coupon and present it for payment. The total amount of municipals issued each year ranges around $70 billion; most of it is of the long-term variety.

The great appeal of municipals to investors is that they are exempt from federal taxation with respect to the interest earned on them.

INSTITUTIONAL INVESTORS AS BUYERS OF SERVICES

Contrary to what seems to be a popular misconception, institutional investors are not the major holders of publicly issued securities. Individual shareholders own the greatest chunk of securities outstanding, over $1.3 trillion worth compared to about $1 trillion for all types of institutions—bank trust departments, insurance companies, pension funds, investment companies, mutual savings banks, common trust funds, non-profit foundations, and educational endowments.

The impact of institutional investors on the securities market is much greater than that of individual investors—especially in the short and intermediate terms. The principal reason is that the average institution's pool of assets under management far outweighs that of the average individual investor—plus the fact that the institutions' movements in and out of the market are much easier to follow.

There are about 600,000 pension and welfare plans in the U.S.

Some are large; others are medium-sized; and others range in size from $500,000 to $1.5 million or $2 million in assets under management.

In March, 1979, there was an intriguing report in the *Wall Street Journal*. Equitable Life, one of the largest assurance societies in the U.S., reportedly had sold off $500 million (right, $½ billion) in stocks in advance of the October 1978, free-fall of the stock market. Most of the selling was in August, September, and early October—before the bombs fell on the stock market.

Two points are observable here:

- Most acute perception of the stock market is best described as happening by chance. The Equitable managers were selling in the late summer-early autumn weeks because they had a need for current funds to pay policy-holder dividends, according to a spokesman.
- The funds realized from the sale of stocks went into bonds—a mix of high yielding items—just in time to catch the capital markets in one of its interest-rate cartwheels.

Suppose that Equitable, its need to switch being more compelling, had decided to unload $½ billion worth of stocks, let's say in 24 hours—or a week for that matter, with a total equity portfolio exceeding $3 billion, then and there the earth would have been shaking almost instantaneously in trading marts all over the country. If the big insurance combine had not spaced its switch out of stocks and into bonds over two months, it might well have precipitated a strong reaction in an already highly nervous stock market.

As it was, other institutional investors were aware that Equitable was doing some switching, but the ultimate size of the move was not apparent. If it had been, it might well have touched off a selling panic. Something similar happened in 1974 when great numbers of large institutions tried to exit the revolving door at the same time.

It's obvious that the institutional investors are the real major leaders in the investment parade. Individual investors have been net sellers of stocks since the sixties, and the institutions net buyers. But there also have been changes within changes.

Until the mid-sixties, the average portfolio mix of the non-restricted institutional investor (e.g., a mutual fund), heavily favored equities. A typical ratio might be 70-75 percent in stocks, 20 percent or so in bonds, and the remainder in cash. With the stock market on the rise, life for the institutional portfolio manager, while neither as idyllic nor as serene as a sell side counterpart might pretend, still was comparatively complacent. Compared to what was to happen from the mid-sixties onward, it was extremely complacent indeed.

A PAIR OF MAJOR CHANGES

Two developments hit the securities industry in the 1965-1974 decade with devastating force: inflation and ERISA (an acronym for the Employee Retirement Income Security Act, explained on page 46).

Although inflation was not widely recognized as a powerful imbalancing force that was pushing the U.S. economy dangerously off course before the late sixties, the water actually began rising in the hold from 1966 onward. Such indices as the consumer price index, wholesale commodity prices, and interest rates began to move ominously upward in response to the guns-and-butter demands on the nation's productive capacity.

Life for the institutional investor began to change from relative calm to frantic frenzy with the fails disasters in 1967-1968 and the sharp stock market decline in 1968-1970. Although there was a temporary respite in the market's recovery in 1971-1972, a drastic change erupted in 1973-1974, when the spurious speculative enthusiasm of the go-go money managers exploded with a nauseating bang. This phenomenon was closely allied with dougle-digit inflation. Their combined effect brought the stock market—and institutional money managers virtually without exception—to their knees.

Before inflation ran wild in 1973-1974, the governing principle in all securities markets was the very logical risk/reward ratio. This concept, from the days of the buttonwood brokers onward, decreed that the greater the potential risk, the greater the potential reward.

Stocks had higher risk/reward ratios because investors did not have their risks minimized by any legal commitments by the stock issuers that their investments would be repaid or that they would otherwise be rewarded, except as claims on the residual assets of the issuing corporations should they go bankrupt. Of course, investors expected to make money by buying stocks in the form of price appreciation—i.e., the market values of the stocks would rise commensurate with the improved performance of the issuing corporations. They usually expected to receive some return in the form of dividends paid by the issuers to their stockholders. It was understood, however, that there was no legal assurance or commitment that either of these reward factors would materialize. Thus the risk to the investors in stocks was higher, and the potential rewards greater, than to the investors in bonds.

The bondholders were protected by several legal covenants that gave them maximum assurance their investments would be repaid and that they would also receive periodic rewards for the use of their funds in the form of interest payments. Unlike the stockholders, however, the bondholders were assured nothing more than repayment of the face value of the debt securities they had invested in, whereas the price of the stockholders' equities could go upward without limit. The basic principle was clear. The risk/reward ratio of an equity investment was higher than that of a debt investment.

Inflation Changes the Market

Double-digit inflation in the 1970s turned this historic investment concept completely upside down. With the cost of living rising at a much faster clip than their puchasing power, the

John Q. Publics awoke to a horrible reality: their own private economy was rolling downhill toward the edge of a cliff. The public didn't merely protest; it shouted that someone had better do something constructive at once. Disaster seemed imminent!

The Federal Reserve System slammed on the monetary brakes with both feet. Interest rates went through the windshield—and the roof. A bank prime rate of 12 percent became a fact of life. Yields of more than 10 percent became available on U.S. government bonds, the world's safest security. Where was there any potential reward like that in the equity market, particularly when the stock market was rapidly declining? The New York Stock Exchange Index at the end of 1972 was 64.48; at the end of 1973 it was 51.82; and at the end of 1974, 36.13. A 44 percent drop in two years represented the greatest decline since the Depression period forty years earlier. Where was the bottom—the bottom of the sea? The traditional risk/reward ratio was turned upside down.

Distress on the Pension Front: Enter ERISA

The hundreds of billions of dollars in losses from the pension, welfare, and retirement funds managed by institutional investors—as well as the individual investors' own losses—raised a nationwide hue and cry for protective legislation. Out of Congress there emerged the Employee Retirement Income Security Act of 1974—quickly shortened on Wall Street to ERISA.

The initial impetus for ERISA came from the conglomerate era of the sixties, when thousands of corporate mergers resulted in the abrupt terminations of innumerable pension plans. During the merger frenzy of the sixties, the reason for wiping out the pension plans of acquired companies usually was attributed to "economic reality." The denial or reduction of pension benefits for merged employees totaled almost $200 million.

It should be made clear that except in a remarkably few instances, there was no embezzlement or fraud on the part of the money managers supervising the hundreds of billions of dollars in assets that took such an horrendous beating in the 1968-1974 period.

The ultimate result was to give an extremely sharp point and cutting edge to ERISA when it became law in 1974.

ERISA is truly revolutionary legislation that is bound to have a profound effect on the securities industry as long as it exists. Since it is virtually a totally new dimension for the industry, it brings with it a whole new array of career opportunities for those interested in the investment markets.

Before ERISA, the management of private pension funds was controlled by state-administered trust laws. ERISA has pre-empted existing state laws and regulations and has raised a nationwide regulatory umbrella over all aspects of private pension fund management.

While the chief focal point of ERISA is private pension funds, it also has important provisions for self-employed individuals who must finance their own retirement plans. The new legislation enlarges the tax-exempt provisions of Keogh plan participations from $2,500 to $7,500 annually (and a further enlargment now seems to be in the works). For other individuals not covered by pension or Keogh plans, it enables them through the Individual Retirement Act (IRA) to set aside portions of their income as tax-sheltered retirement pools.

For the registered representatives with the sell side securities firms, these aspects of the ERISA legislation package open broad new avenues of revenue-producing opportunities. The overall impact of ERISA has been felt most forcefully by the institutional investors on the buy side of the wholesale securities markets. Three requirements may be examined to illustrate this effect:

- ERISA mandates that corporate pension officers exercise full prudence and caution in supervising the pension fund assets under their jurisdiction. This includes the selection of outside professional money managers, and the constant monitoring of their performance. The guidelines for the corporate pension officers are to assure that: (a) "prudent" investment policies are being followed including the diversification of securities purchased and the quality of securities acquired; (b) the creation of strategic portfolio plans, and the implementation of these plans, to assure that optimum financial returns are being realized in behalf of the employees and their beneficiaries participating in the pension and other welfare and retirement plans.

Confronted with such pressing needs, corporate managements have been shifting immense amounts of pension funds among the thousands of institutional investors—large and small. A corporate pension officer no longer feeds Nephew Charley a big slice of the pension pool because Charley is with ABC Money Management—and for good reason. Unless Nephew Charley can produce optimum financial returns, his uncle at the client corporation may soon find himself mailing out resumés.

- ERISA requires that employers must disclose fully to employees their funding policies for pension and other retirement plans, and to update these reports regularly. Employees, especially members of unions in the big industrial corporations, have formed their own monitoring committees. This, in turn, has caused corporate managements to scrutinize more closely the performance results of outside money managers hired to plan and implement portfolio investment strategies.

Institutional investors have their money management results posted continuously on a scoreboard. The money managers now must meet at least quarterly with their corporate clients and review the hits, runs, and errors of the previous innings—and what they plan to do in the next innings to meet the goals and requirements set by the

corporate clients. Not enough hits and runs, or too many errors, and the corporate client moves his business elsewhere. The shifting of corporate pension funds elsewhere among institutional money managers has increased by at least one thousand percent in the last five years.
- The ERISA requirement that all possible prudence be exercised in the investment of pension funds has resulted in the dramatic shift of the traditional equity/debt ratios that obtained in the pre-seventies. Where once a 70-30 percent ratio was the norm, it has now shifted to something like 50-50—and is still heading down.

Shifting to bonds thus is the direction of many money managers on the buy side. One of them, a seasoned professional, reports that many corporations are instructing their outside money managers to limit equity investment to 10 percent, instead of going to the usual 50 percent or 60 percent of total funds available.

Returning to the more traditional ratios will await the time when inflation rates come down, and when their wayward companion, interest rates, simultaneously or subsequently are reduced, according to this observer.

Will such conditions occur in the foreseeable future? Will the risk/reward ratio ever be rightside up again? Have ERISA and competitive commission rates permanently changed the direction in which the buy side of the investment world spins? The answers await future developments in many quarters of the overall economy—nationally *and* worldwide.

Overleaf: Two fingers indicate the round lots an options trader will purchase at the going price. (Marty Cobin Photography.)

CHAPTER 5

THE BUY SIDE OF THE RETAIL MARKET

The millions of individual investors who directly manage their own securities investments comprise the buy side of the retail market. This of course does not mean John Doe races out on to the floor of the Big Board crying, "I want to buy 100 GM." Nor does it mean Jane Doe scoots out on the floor of the Amex yelling, "I want to sell 100 Washington Post."

RELIANCE UPON STOCKBROKERS

What's more, very few individuals have the ability to say or do the right thing when dealing directly in over-the-counter transactions. Unlike the Big Board, the Amex and the other half dozen major exchanges, the OTC market does not have a physical plant. In effect, it's a collection of telephone or teletype terminals that link brokerage firms and market-makers who trade in OTC stocks—meaning those not listed on the exchanges.

So the millions of individuals who manage their own investment portfolios, themselves, still use the broker/dealer firms as intermediaries. The individuals, with or without the advice of their stockbrokers, decide on what they will buy or sell and the brokerage firms complete the transactions.

MANY REASONS TO BUY OR SELL SECURITIES

The principal merchandise, for which the individual investor shops in the securities markets, is incremental purchasing power. When you get right down to it, that's what money means to most people: purchasing power. Save it, and it means future purchasing power. When John Q. Public has funds to spare, he can put them in a savings account where they become a collective chunk of purchasing power accruing incremental value through the payment of interest on his savings.

An alternative is to invest this surplus in securities. A person buys a security because he or she has identified it as potentially having more incremental value—and also more risk—than a savings deposit. One sells a security because either: (a) it's achieved the investment objective—e.g., a 20 percent increase in market value over what was paid for it; (b) the person gets the sad message that his or her investment objective of price appreciation with dividend payments is not going to be achieved; (c) one needs liquid purchasing power for one reason or another; or (d) the person has identified what seems to be a better opportunity elsewhere to add to the purchasing power of the invested funds.

Much controversial opinion has been published in recent years about "the flight of individual investors from the securities markets." Advocates of this point of view often cite the latest survey of individual shareholders taken by the New York Stock Exchange. The most recent count showed that in 1975 the number of individual shareholders had dropped to about 25 million from an all-time high of 30 million in 1970.

There's no reason to question the fact that the population of individual stockowners has declined substantially in the seventies. John and Jane Doe, after all, during the speculative sixties and early seventies, took severe losses in managing their own portfolios. Without exception, individuals were sellers while the market was rising and buyers when it was going down. Adding to this grievous disillusionment was the horrendous performance of the professional money managers in the late sixties and early seventies (1973-1974 particularly)—i.e., the pros who were supposed to be preserving the individuals' store of purchasing power in their pension, welfare, and retirement funds.

NEW TYPES OF SECURITIES

Understandably, then, individuals deserted the stock markets in droves during the past decade. This doesn't mean for a moment that they deserted all other areas of the investment markets as well. Quite to the contrary, the current aggregates of individuals' securities holdings show that individuals have more funds invested in securities than ever before. The types of securities favored by individual investors have undergone marked changes, however.

Fixed-Income Mutual Funds

One example of how the individual investor has changed horses can be seen in recent developments in mutual funds.

A current headline out of Washington proclaims: "MUTUAL FUND ASSETS RISE TO PEAK" "Net assets of mutual funds rose 1.3 percent to a record $60.6 billion last month..."

Only after reading the full report does one get the real significance of the fundamental changes that have been taking place in the retail market:

- The rise of the net assets in the mutual funds had nothing to do with individuals pooling more of their savings for equity investments.
- Net assets in mutual funds in the form of equity investments have continued to fall at an annual rate of 20 percent according to recent tabulations.
- The number of individuals who have invested in fixed-income funds in 1979 was 639,000, up from 193,000 in little more than a year.

- The amount of funds individuals have invested in fixed-income (money market) funds has jumped to more than $25 billion from less than $1 billion in 1974.

Thus: MUTUAL FUNDS RISE TO PEAK

For an even more convincing indication of how the sell side of Wall Street has reacted to the new directions of individuals in pursuing incremental value on their securities investments, one has only to read the opening paragraphs of a prospectus (See Glossary.) offered individuals recently in promoting a new mutual fund to be distributed by one of the largest brokerage firms.

It reads:

> "The Fund is a diversified open-end investment company whose primary objective is to maximize current income. The Fund intends to invest in a diversified portfolio of fixed-income securities, such as corporate bonds and notes, convertible securities, preferred stocks and government obligations which the Investment Advisor believes will offer high yields without undue risk. As a secondary objective, the Fund will seek capital appreciation when consistent with its primary objective.... The Fund expects to seek high current income by investing principally in fixed-income securities which are *not* rated in the higher rating categories of the established rating services. Such securities ordinarily will be rated below A by Moody's Investors Service and Standard and Poor's, or will be unrated securities of comparable quality.

The Fund, introduced in November of 1978, in the succeeding nine months acquired $176 million in assets under management from more than 20,000 shareholders. The prospectus cited above is a dramatic departure from the former mutual fund promotions that stressed the growth potential in "a well diversified portfolio of common stocks." In the seventies a whole new crop of investment company alternatives has been devised by the sell side securities firms to take advantage of the individual's focus on fixed-income securities as the most promising form of investment in view of the stock market's inflation-ridden chronic illness.

Besides the relatively new types of fixed-income mutual funds, individuals also have a supermarket spread of other investment instruments to choose from, that were put on the shelves by the big sell side securities firms in the seventies.

Unit Trusts

These include either single investment vehicles such as a special issue of corporate bonds or preferred stocks especially designed to attract individuals, or—and much more frequently—new packages of a variety of securities of the same or different categories labeled as "unit investment trusts," or simply, "unit trusts."

A unit trust is somewhat like a mutual fund except that it is organized and marketed espectially as a short-to-intermediate-term investment package and sells shares to individuals in a fixed portfolio usually of fixed-income securities. Once these shares are sold, no additional shares are marketed in that particular unit trust—although, one may rest assured, there will be a wide variety of other unit trusts coming on the market as long as short-term interest rates remain unusually high. In the event of a return to interest-rate normality, provisions usually are included in unit trusts to convert holdings in those trusts to longer-term investment pools distributed by the same sponsoring sell side firm.

The particular appeal of the unit trust for individuals is that it offers a convenient method of participating, for as little as $1,000 a share, in such otherwise high-minimum-entrance-cost instruments as bonds, preferred stocks, government securities, or certificates of deposits.

The typical unit trust offers the investor not only a diversified collection of preferred stocks or bonds, but also a pool of securities with different maturities and yields. The trust normally pays dividends or interest to its shareholders on either a monthly, quarterly, or semi-annual basis. One of the latest features of some of the newer forms of these trusts is to offer participants the opportunity of writing checks (usually called something like "drafts") on whatever cash values have been built up for participants as the unit trust matures.

Some of the more common forms of unit trusts now being widely marketed include:

Certificate of Deposit Trusts. These have become increasingly popular since the advent of the era of high interest rates, particularly with short-term oriented investors. Certificate of Deposit trusts ordinarily have a life span of no more than six months. The portfolio of a CD trust consists of a number of certificates of deposit originating from different commercial banks. Instead of periodic payments of interest, interest is accumulated over the life of the trust and paid to the shareholders when the trust is terminated, at which time principal also is paid.

Government Guaranteed Securities Trusts. Unit trusts of this sort are composed of securities guaranteed by Uncle Sam or his agencies. They consist largely of Ginnie Maes and usually offer top-dollar in interest payments because of the ordinarily higher interest paid to mortgage lenders.

Corporate Bond Trusts. Portfolios in trusts of this sort consist of a fixed group of corporate debt securities purchased initially for each trust. They usually remain in the portfolio until maturity or until they are called (principal prepaid) by the issuer. The sponsors of a corporate trust bond customarily maintain secondary markets for trust units. But individuals primarily regard this sort of investment as something to be held to maturity even though the sponsor usually is legally obliged to redeem an individual's unit holdings when units are presented for redemption. The amount of payment will depend on the value of the bonds at the time of redemption, plus any interest accrued.

Municipal Bond Trusts. These trusts operate quite similarly to the corporate bond trusts except that the interest earned is exempt from federal taxation. However, the individual unit holder can incur a taxable capital gain (or loss) should the sponsor dispose of one or more of the municipals in the portfolio—for one or more of a variety of reasons. Most trusts give the sponsor/trustee the right to change elements of the portfolio should changing market or economic conditions threaten the stability of the municipal issues concerned.

Preferred Stock Trusts. While thousands of individual investors invest large parts of their surplus purchasing power in this type of trust, they are of special interest to corporate investors because 85 percent of the dividends (as contrasted to the interest paid on the bond trusts) are tax-exempt for corporations. For individuals, too, since income is in the form of dividends, the first $100 also is tax exempt—assuming the individual has no other income from dividend payments.

Options More Popular

Although most individual investors in recent years have been shying away from the traditional investment avenues of equity acquisition, there has been one development related to the stock market that has shown phenomenal expansion: options.

An option is the right to buy or sell 100 shares of a particular stock at a particular price by a particular date. A *put* is the right to sell it, and a *call* the right to buy it.

Both puts and calls by their nature are highly speculative forms of investment—highly speculative being the Wall Street euphemism for highly risky. Before 1973, only a relatively few brokers/ dealers specializing in options offered this type of investment opportunity. These specialist firms essentially would bet on the laws of probability that the buyer of a put or a call (their prices varied according to the underlying stocks and the strike, or exercise, price and expirations dates) would be wrong in the market price change anticipated at the time the put or call was bought.

The volume of options sold by the broker/dealer specialist firms under the old system of investing in puts-and-calls was very modest, possibly no more than a few thousand contracts each month for the securities industry as a whole.

In 1973, however, came the revolution. The options market went public when the Chicago Board Options Exchange (CBOE) was organized. The CBOE neither buys nor sells options and does not establish option prices. In this sense, it functions similarly to the New York Stock Exchange in terms of the stocks listed on the Big Board. The CBOE—and more recently the American Options Exchange, a latter day competitor organized by the American Stock Exchange—provide the place, the facilities, and the ground rules that enable buyers and sellers of options to do business.

The growth of the options business, since it went public in 1973, has been one of the wonders of the investment age. In 1974, for example, public trading in options aggregated to 40,000 transactions a day—a vast increase over the daily volume under the old broker/dealer system, but only a meek forerunner of what was on the way. Current volume on the options exchanges exceeds 200,000 trades daily. What's more, since each option represents a claim against 100 shares of the underlying stock, the implicit trading volume of options transactions amounts to about 20 million shares—equivalent to a good day's total volume on the Big Board. The New York Stock Exchange, incidentally, has been backing and filling about opening its own options exchange for the past four or five years. Currently, it seems to be awaiting the outcome of an in-depth investigation by the SEC which is trying to determine what, if any, impact options trading has on securities trading generally.

Although options trading probably has attracted the most attention among the new investment techniques available to individuals, it doesn't change the underlying fact that the public, as individuals, has been investing much larger proportions of its purchasing power than ever before in capital market and money market instruments (other than the traditional bond or stock securities).

Other Investment Possibilities

A shopping list of the new investment instruments available to individuals, along with the unit trusts described earlier, would include:

Assets Management	Floating rate notes
Bankers acceptances	Index futures
Commercial paper	Insurance plans
Commodities	Keogh and IRA plans
Comprehensive financial planning	Option mutual funds
Deep-discount bonds	Tax-free notes
Financial futures	Tax-sheltered investments

For that matter, there are thousands of people who have remained awake and at work in the securities industry during these years who still find it difficult to believe the evidence right there before their eyes.

For some people, unfortunately, change means only problems, often insurmountable. For others, luckily, change means opportunities, often golden.

Overleaf: One major area of the wholesale market is that of government securities.

CHAPTER 6

THE SELLING SIDE OF THE WHOLESALE MARKET

Wall Street, where paradoxes of all sorts abound, has seen its most notable "contradiction" develop on the selling side of the securities markets. On the one hand, expansion has occurred in the number of so-called "products" (although in fact they are all services), marketed by the major securities firms. On the other hand, there has been a significant "compression," or reduction, in the number of securities firms in the industry. For example, the number of member firms on the Big Board dropped by approximately 20 percent in the 1969-1978 decade. In May, 1978, *Fortune* published tabulated data under the headline, "The Big 25, a List You've Never Seen Before." But while the number of registered sell side firms was shrinking, the merger waves of the 1960s and 1970s increased immensely the service dimensions of the leading investment-service providers.

In a five-year span (1972-1977), the total capital of the Big 25 had jumped by more than 50 percent, despite multimillion dollars of investments in technology to keep pace with the avalanche of trading and transactions volume that concurrently kept rolling over the securities firms. This was during the greatest growth decade in volume in the history of the securities industry. In 1969 the daily average of stock shares traded was 11.4 million; in 1978 it was 28.5 million. Bond volume trading expanded almost geometrically, reflecting the investment community's retreat from new equity issues and its new emphasis upon fixed-income securities as an anti-inflation protective measure. As the new decade of the seventies drew to a close in 1979, both stock and bond volume trend lines were still climbing toward new highs.

Before the enormous expansion era following World War II, Wall Street was similar to a collection of specialty shops. There were the investment banks that traditionally originated the undewriting of securities for corporate clients; the big nationwide wire houses that were the principal distributors of securities to the investing public; the firms that specialized in bond issues; and there were the smaller firms whose specialty was research. These were all distinctive components of the selling side of the securities business.

THE RISE OF SECURITIES "SUPERMARKETS"

One of the most surprising developments was the consolidation of the selling side of the wholesale markets from the 1950s to the 1970s. The loose collections of specialty shops have now been integrated into supermarkets. Most of the Big 25 have become full-service financial services companies, providing services to individual, institutional, and corporate investors as brokers and dealers in corporate and municipal securities, as investment bankers heavily involved in underwriting, as brokers in commodities and financial futures contracts, as assets managers, and as agents in selling the other services in the ever-increasing product lines.

The relatively new giant "supermarkets" on the *Fortune* list of the Big 25 now employ about 100,000 people, 40 percent more than only five years ago. None of these full-service firms have a payroll of less than 1,000 and just about all of them have annual gross revenues approaching $100 million or more. In the aggregate, their gross revenues in 1977, according to the *Fortune* survey, were in excess of $3.3 billion.

The Big 25 ring up well over half of all the revenues garnered every year by the securities industry. They originate and distribute at least 75 percent of all the securities marketed in the capital-formation process. The securities industry today then, with respect to most of the revenues and profits generated by the sell side, no longer is a collection of relatively small business partnerships. It is big business in every sense of the term.

A MAJOR SELL SIDE ACTIVITY: INVESTMENT BANKING

One of the principal functions integrated into the modern full-service firm is investment banking. It is the well-head source of almost all sell side revenues derived from the services sold to wholesale customers. Investment banking, in its most commonplace connotation, is a synonym for underwriting: the process whereby a securities firm buys part or all of a securities issue from a corporation or government body for resale to the public. At first glance, this would seem to be a relatively simple relationship: the investment banker is a middle-man who sells the use of funds from those who have them in surplus to those who have a need for their use.

Essentially, there are four stages in the process: (1) the preliminaries; (2) the "deal"—the agreement; (3) the legalities; and (4) the "moment of truth"—approval and terms. Each will be discussed in turn.

The Preliminaries. The initial phase of an underwriting will differ from others according to the following variables: whether it's the first issue of securities for public sale in the capital markets; the amount of capital to be raised; the financial structure and earnings record of the borrower; and a number of additional factors involving the history of the issuing corporation, the quality and reputation of its management, and the issuer's connections and general savoir-faire with respect to the investment community.

Let's assume for the sake of brevity and clarity that a public corporation, Public Corporation, Inc. (or PCI), wants to raise between $15 and $20 million in the capital markets. We'll assume, too, that PCI, the issuer, is a seasoned issuer—as most big companies are. Its principal investment banker is Universal Capital Corp. (UCC), with whom the issuer has developed a close relationship over the years. In short, it will be a negotiated debt issue.

By far the greatest volume of capital raised by publicly held corporations is through debt issues rather than through the sale of stock. In fact, this applies in general terms throughout the spectrum of borrowers in the capital markets. For every dollar of corporate equity marketed each year, at least four dollars of debt are sold. (This has resulted in economists pinning a variety of labels on the U.S. economy. Those of friendly persuasion call it "highly leveraged"; others refer to it as "dangerously debt-ridden.")

In periods of high inflation, especially when stock prices seem to be caught in quicksand, most corporate borrowers prefer the comparatively certain results of issuing debt rather than the many uncertainties surrounding an issue of equity.

For this and other reasons of a similar nature, PCI, the client/issuer, and UCC, its investment bank/financial advisor, come to a quick meeting of the minds. They decide on a new $20 million issue of 20-year bonds—specifically, general obligation bonds. This hopefully will enable the issue to be marketed at 100 percent of the price with an interest rate reflecting its expected BBB rating by Standard & Poor's, and an equivalent Ba evaluation by Moody's.

Standard & Poor's and Moody's are the two major rating services that separately analyze the issuer's ability to meet interest payments in full, when due, and to pay back the principal when the bonds mature. A BBB (Ba) rating in effect tells investors that while the proposed issue is not going to be top quality (AAA or Aaa) it still will be of reasonably good quality. Other things being equal, the level of this rating affects the level of interest payment the issuer will have to offer to assure its 100 percent-priced bonds will be marketed successfully.

Depending on economic conditions and trends in the market for fixed-income securities, an issuer may decide to market its bonds at say 99.5 percent of their face value rather than at 100 percent. This permits a lower interest coupon to be affixed to the bonds. Investors thus have an opportunity to buy the securities for less than their maturity value. This increases the yield investors receive to approximately the same level that would have been available from a 100 percent-priced issue with a higher interest coupon.

How the issue is priced, an approximation of the amount of interest it will pay, and the timing of the issue's entrance into the markets are only a very few of the many decisions the issuer will make in conjunction with its principal investment bank in the preliminary phase of a securities issue. Even though the role of the investment bank now has become less dominant in the preliminary decision-making stage of a negotiated issue than in earlier years, it remains a key role nevertheless.

Although most corporate issues are negotiated, competitive bidding is an alternative method of underwriting used occasionally for industrial issues under special circumstances. For example, a sizable company that decides to tap the capital markets for the first time often submits a prospective issue to a number of potential underwriters. The underwriters send in sealed bids separately that remain secret until they are opened simultaneously on a specified date. The winning bid is that which offers the highest price to the issuer.

Competitive bidding is optional for the industrial corporate issuer, but it is mandated by law or regulation for many public utility and government issues, including government agencies. Although it might appear that it would be to the advantage of all issuers to tap the capital markets via competitive bidding, by no means is this the case.

Because of the complexities of engineering a major financing, an issuing corporation will usually retain an investment bank acting in an advisory role. Although competitive bidding is not the avenue most frequently followed, when it is recommended, as in the case of tax-exempt securities, for example, the offer will often be shaped with the assistance of an investment bank before being put out for bids.

Most large industrial issuers favor negotiated underwriting because of the numerous ways in which investment banks can be of assistance. Initially, the managing underwriter can advise the issuer on the amount of funds needed and the best method of raising the funds in the capital markets—i.e., through a broad distribution or tailoring the issue to fit a special group. The investment bank also can advise the issuer in the preliminary phase of the probable effect of the type of issue selected on the capital structure of the issuer—and how it could affect ratings of future issues.

The managing underwriter also can relieve the issuer of much of the "nuts and bolts" work involved in getting the securities marketed. How much of this burden the managing underwriter, and the group of co-managers enlisted, will shoulder is specified in the underlying agreement between the issuer and the underwriters, often referred to on Wall Street as "The Deal."

The "Deal" the Agreement. The specifics of the underwriting of the $20 million issue of bonds for PCI must be clearly spelled out by the managing investment bank for the other members of the underwriting syndicate. It is only after there is a 100 percent accord among all the syndicate participants that a contract, legally referred to as the "agreement among underwriters," can be signed (usually on the date the registration of the issue becomes effective).

The agreement or deal specifies the price that the underwriting syndicate will pay the issuer for the issue and the kind of contract the manager is authorized to sign. After the agreement among the syndicate of underwriters is signed, the manager then can sign the overall contract on behalf of the whole syndicate with the issuer.

The Legalities. The contract between the issuer and underwriters specifies which of the preliminary legal requirements will be handled by the underwriters as obligations to the issuer. Let's assume that UCC in behalf of the underwriting syndicate has agreed to help prepare the prospectus, the registration statement, and the supporting documents, and will help insure compliance with the requirements of the regulatory authorities.

The Securities and Exchange Commission is the principal legal tribunal whose screening of a public issue of securities is an essential prerequisite to marketing the securities. This screening process is completed only after all the required information has been filed and reviewed by the SEC. In the contract between the UCC and the PCI, the managing underwriter is committed to this responsibility.

The registration of a sizable issue with the SEC requires the accumulation and forwarding of voluminous information about the issuer and the nature and manner of distribution of the securities. After these filing requirements have been met, and while these documents are under review, the underwriters begin warming up the market.

They do this largely by circulating a preliminary prospectus known as a "red herring." This is chiefly an information summary of the forthcoming issue except for the omission of final details such as the price, interest rate (or number of shares if it is stock), and the spread (meaning the amount the underwriters will receive and the net proceeds to the issuer).

A red herring is so named because the preliminary prospectus has a warning on the front page printed in red ink. This warning states that the preliminary prospectus is not an offer whereby the securities under review by the SEC can be bought or sold. The marketing of the issue can proceed only after the SEC renders its final go-ahead.

However, the preliminary prospectus is an extremely useful device for the underwriting syndicate and sales departments of the distributing firms. It enables them to test the market and to generate preliminary interest in the offering before the SEC gives it a green light.

The Moment of Truth—Approval and Terms. This advance effort is especially useful in deciding on the optimum price and other terms of the issue when the moment of truth arrives—i.e., the day the SEC gives the final go-ahead and the underwriters set the offering price and spread.

Although the terms of issues vary widely in precise details, more often than not they reflect three fundamental factors: the quality of the securities, the yields offered investors compared with generally similar investment opportunities, and demand/supply conditions in the capital markets (in turn reflecting to a considerable degree general economic conditions).

THREE ACTUAL OFFERINGS

Three examples of security issues summarized below include actual offerings that were successfully marketed in the second half of 1979.

The first issue was an issue of $60 million in bonds, at an interest rate of 12 percent, due in 1999. The terms of the first offering were:

	Price (1) to Public	Underwriting Discounts and Commissions (2)	Proceeds to Company (3)
Per Bond	100.00%	2.20%	97.80%
Total	$60,000,000	$1,320,000	$58,680,000

The second example is an issue of 905,000 shares of common stock of a retail chain. Shown below are the terms for this second example.

	Price to Public	Underwriting Discounts and Commissions	Proceeds to Selling Shareholders
Per Share	$13.00	$.77	$12.23
Total	$11,765,000	$696,850	$11,068,150

The third example is an offering of "Units," or packages consisting of one part debt and one part equity. Each unit in this instance consisted of one debenture with a principal of $1,000 and 60 shares of common stock. After the initial marketing of the Units, the debentures would be convertible into common shares on the basis of $10.75 per share (equivalent to approximately 93 shares of common stock for each $1,000 principal amount of debentures). The terms: ($10,000,000 9% Convertible Subordinated Debentures due in 1994 with 600,000 shares of Common Stock)

	Price to Public	Underwriting Discounts	Proceeds to the Company
Per Unit	$1,547.50	$96.00	$1,451.50
Total	$15,475,000	$960,000	$14,515,000

The three examples of underwritings summarized above only hint at the innumerable transformations involved in bringing thousands of debt and equity issues of securities to the capital markets each year. Given the volatility of security prices, the constant changes in demand/supply conditions in the capital markets, and the unpredictability of future economic conditions, there is no such thing as a "model" underwriting. Every security issue in a sense is unique, tailored to fit the needs of the issuer in the context of constantly changing capital market conditions, and to provide the securities firms involved with a reasonable profit for their considerable contributions.

A security issue that is priced too low will sell very readily in the markets. However, it will not return an optimum price to the issuer. The next time the issuer comes to market, it well may be under the management of a different investment banker.

A security issue that is priced too high will be very rewarding for the issuer when the underwriters buy it. If the price is out of line with competitive issues in the market, however, the underwriters will be unable to distribute it—and will have to digest the loss themselves. Too many unrealistic pricing decisions can mean financial disaster for the underwriters involved. Consequently, investment banking, given the high state of flux that surrounds it on all sides, is a constant challenge for those who choose it as a career. Commercial banks also fill important roles in the underwriting and marketing of municipal issues, and both commercial banks and investment banks are principal conduits for marketing federal government securities.

A SECOND MAJOR AREA: GOVERNMENT SECURITIES

As outlined in Chapter 5, the federal government and federal agencies use a variety of securities in raising the capital needed to finance the cost of running the government and to support some non-government activities in the economy considered to be of significance to government economic policy.

The total amount of federal securities issued annually recently has been between $40 billion and $50 billion net, not including federal agency financings.

As in market transactions for all securities, there are two phases of marketing U.S. securities: primary marketing and secondary marketing. The first involves bringing new issues into the markets; the second involves trading the securities after they have been introduced.

The U.S. Treasury decides when new issues will be offered and at what price. These issues are sold on a subscription basis to the full gamut of investors—Federal Reserve and commercial banks, institutional and individual investors.

Although Treasury issues are listed on the New York Stock Exchange, they are traded over-the-counter by a select group of between thirty and forty government dealers. Government securities dealers of primary stature are an elite group who operate under a special set of ground rules. For example, while municipal and corporate securities' price changes are measured in basis points and 1/8 of a dollar respectively, government securities' prices are quoted in 32nds. Another distinction is that while most broker/dealer firms act chiefly as brokers in transactions involving municipal and corporate securities, in the government securities market, transactions revolve around dealers acting for their own accounts.

MARKET STRATEGIES OF THE EXPANDED FIRMS

"Securities are not bought, they are sold," is an ancient investment maxim that has special significance, in this era of institutionalization of the securities business, for institutional sales forces of the big supermarket firms. Many of the former wire houses, which concentrated on the retail market, acquired sales personnel with wholesale experience as a result of consolidation. The large retail firms with relatively large capital bases acquired many of the small "research boutiques" that had concentrated on selling their analytical output to institutional investors. The sales efforts by the boutiques were handled either by analyst-salesmen or by a pairing of an analyst with a salesman as a team.

Most of the big sell side firms have organized their institutional selling efforts as separate sales staffs apart from their research departments. The typical big sell side firm divides its institutional market geographically with groups of salesmen covering each regional area. Often, an institutional sales force will be further divided into equity and fixed-income specialists, although the total effort, more often than not, will be under the direction of a single national sales manager.

Many of the full-service firms have a two-tier strategy for building up order flow from the wholesale side of the markets. Approximately $300 million in commission revenues is derived from institutional investors each year by the Big 25 sell side firms. By far the greatest amount of this commission revenue comes from the 300 or so largest institutional investors—the big insurance companies, commercial bank trust departments, mutual fund complexes, and pension fund managers.

The sell side supermarkets, quite naturally, concentrate their distribution and order-flow expansion efforts first on the top-tier 300 institutions and then on the second-tier money managers of lesser size.

Most of the big institutions direct the major part of their commission business to varying groups of ten to twelve of the full-service securities firms. The compensation consists of "soft dollars"—i.e., commissions paid for research, trading, positioning, or other services provided by the sell side firms.

The competition among the Big 25 supermarkets to retain their market shares, or expand their shares, of institutional business has become exceedingly fierce. The advent of competitive bidding and negotiated rates for institutional commission business on May 1, 1975 (commonly called Mayday—See Glossary.), has squeezed the profit-margins on this source of revenues to the point where they have become wafer-thin. Since all sell side firms regard their share of the institutional market as both an important prestige factor and a vital component of other more profitable services, the competition is expected to continue to intensify for a bigger slice of the institutional investor commission market.

Since Mayday, commission revenues have dropped by as much as $600 million from institutional investors, reflecting a decrease in the rates charged by sell side firms now averaging about 45 percent of their former levels. This, in part, has been balanced by an increase in commission revenues from individual investors. More important, from the perspective of the sell side firm's focus on wholesale revenues, has been an increase in revenues from underwriting and from corporate finance services.

As Samuel D. Hayes III has pointed out in the *Harvard Business Review*, the reliance of securities firms on underwriting and corporate finance income has grown incessantly for more than a decade.

"The mix of revenues has shifted significantly since 1966," Professor Hayes says, "when almost 62 percent of securities firms' revenues came from brokerage commissions and only 7.3 percent from underwriting and corporate financial services."

He continues, "At the end of 1977, only 41 percent of securities firms' revenues came from commissions and 11.5 percent came from underwriting/corporate finance."

In other words, the growth in total revenues from the two sources shows the most dramatic change. As Professor Hayes illustrates, while commission income was increasing 62 percent from 1966 to 1977, revenues from underwriting and corporate finance were up 273 percent. These fundamental changes in the wholesale revenue streams of the sell side firms have become even more pronounced in the last three years, according to this writer.

Of comparable importance to the big sell side firms have been the changes in profitability in their various market areas. The profit margins on the services they provide for fees have been much healthier than the profits (if any) derived directly from their institutional commission business. These fee-generating services include private placements, mergers and acquisitions, and financial consulting for government agencies, state and local governments, and of course private corporations.

By the time an originating investment bank, as the lead manager in an underwriting, gets through slicing up the revenue pie with the co-managers and distribution syndicate, the take-home piece can be modestly profitable at best. And then there's the risk involved. If the issue proves to be badly timed or badly priced, or the market collapses in the middle of it, the underwriters can wind up with no profit at all—or even a sizable loss.

OTHER INCOME-PRODUCING ACTIVITIES

An originating investment bank can earn as much as .5 percent on a $100 million private placement. This is risk-free once the terms are set, a process that usually can be completed in much less time than the average underwriting. Since making money is the objective in the securities industry as in all others, it's easy to understand why the private placement business has been one of the major growth targets in revenues *and* profits—for the sell side of the wholesale market.

Even more lucrative have been their numerous roles in corporate mergers and acquisitions (called M/A by a sell side firm's specialists in this area). The wave of corporate mergers and acquisitions has been rolling along at tidal levels in recent years. There have been two primary causes: the unprecedentedly high costs of expanding or modernizing productive plants and equipment owing to inflation; the unprecedentedly low levels of price/earnings ratios over the past decade. Growth-oriented companies with financial muscle have found it cheaper to buy the assets of other companies by acquiring their stock rather than taking the more costly route of new brick-and-mortar construction.

Investment banks work both sides of the M/A street and also can turn a profit in the middle of the street as well. Usually, when a sizable merger takes place, one investment bank will represent the acquiring company while another functions in behalf of the acquiree. In the middle of the street may be one or more other investment banks acting as arbitraguers—buyers or sellers of either or both companies' stock to keep price volatility at a manageable minimum during the merger process. (See Glossary.)

Many M/A deals involve hundreds of millions of dollars, and when these huge rocks are dropped into the lake they cause significant trading undulations. The arbitrageurs keep these waves under control by trading blocks of stock (as either buyers or sellers) when the prices of the acquirer's or acquiree's shares tend to move away from what the investment bank arbitrageurs regard as realistic levels. Without arbitrage, speculation during the merger process could make it very difficult to set the terms for an exchange of the acquirer's shares for those of the acquiree.

Successful arbitrage during a major merger requires an investment bank to have the nerves of a tightrope walker, in-depth experience in evaluating the market impact of the acquisition, a very sophisticated trading desk, and the ability to work closely with the investment banks representing the acquirer or acquiree.

Although there are no results posted by the sell side firms about M/A income specifically (they're part of the catch-all category "Other"), most informed observers believe M/A has been the most profitable wholesale growth area for sell side firms in the seventies.

While the foregoing has focused chiefly on the Big 25 securities firms as all-purpose service providers for wholesale clients, smaller firms outside the major money market centers have managed to survive as independent entities on the sell side of the wholesale market. Actually, as a recent survey indicates, there are scores of smaller firms operating profitably in the money market centers as well—and some of them showing a higher return on equity than their huge competitors.

However, the wave of consolidation among sell side firms has shown few signs of subsiding. As an illustration, among the continuing consolidations of scores of securities firms in the past two years, two mergers involved four of the firms on the Fortune Big 25 list.

Overleaf: By 1970, one out of every four Americans was an individual shareholder and had "bought a piece of America." (Marty Cobin Photography.)

CHAPTER 7

THE SELL SIDE OF THE RETAIL MARKET

Among all the vast changes, which have profoundly altered the securities industry in the past dozen years or so, few have been more significant than the new focus and practices of the big firms that dominate the selling of investment services in the retail market.

The ancient saying that "Securities are not bought, they are sold" is not a full description of how the investment process has been working. It should read: "Securities are not bought, they are sold—and the selling side of the market alone decides which wares will be sold to the buying side."

This, fundamentally, is the way Wall Street has been operating right up to the seventies. It was the method of operating during the two great bull markets of the twentieth century, the first lasting almost a decade in the 1920s and the second lasting even longer, from 1954 to 1969. The selling side—meaning security issuers and their investment bank/brokerage intermediaries—totally controlled the kind and amount of securities supplied to investors. Of course, more recently, the SEC and the National Association of Securities Dealers were there to make sure issuing and trading practices conformed to disclosure and antifraud requirements. The regulators, however, did not participate at all in selecting the type of investments and investment services that characterized the 1954-1969 bull market.

Bull markets always seem to unleash one of the least attractive, but no less enduring, human traits: greed. A sustained upswing in stock prices can be guaranteed to excite the get-rich-quick lust of human beings. The longer a bull market lasts, the greater the number of new investors it attracts.

The 1954-1969 era was the longest bull market in history. Aside from four relatively short periods of classic price corrections, the stock market shot forward in a series of spectacular upward lunges spanning fifteen years. The rush of individual investors into the stock market during this period was chronicled in the following surveys taken by the New York Stock Exchange:

Number of Individual Shareowners

(In Millions)

1952	*1956*	*1959*	*1962*	*1965*	*1970*
6.49	8.63	12.49	17.01	20.12	30.85

The first census showed that approximately one out of 16 adult Americans was an individual shareowner. By 1970, the ratio was one out of four, a remarkable increase.

As 1954 ended, stock prices (as measured by the Dow Jones Industrial Average) pushed past the previous all-time high of 380 that had been set a quarter of a century earlier before the Great Crash of 1929. As 1969 ended, the Dow had penetrated 1,000 and was ranging between 950-1,000; again, a remarkable increase.

"Buy a piece of America" Keith Funston, president of the New York Stock Exchange, had urged during its most spectacular expansion years. By 1970, some 30 million Americans had done just that. At least that's what many of them thought they were doing, although what they were really buying was a piece of the stock market. In any event, in the fifties and sixties the retail market was a sellers' market all the way.

CHANGE TO A BUYERS' MARKET

And there's the rub: it's a market that no longer exists. The great bull market of 1954-1969 is as lifeless as the last dinosaur. Like the dinosaur, a great bull market may never live again.

This pronouncement by no means is universally accepted dogma. Those who uphold it cite the latest census of the Big Board taken in 1975 in support of their position. The 30 million figure of 1970 had shrunk to 25 million by 1975. Some 5 million individual investors in the shares of 11,000 publicly-owned corporations and in several hundred investment companies had fled the equity markets. That was as of mid-1975. And in the interim? Knowledgeable observers, including experts within the Exchange community, generally agree that the attrition of the individual shareowner population in all likelihood has been continuing since the last census. The next head count will be taken by the Exchange later this year (1980). No one will be more surprised than the census-takers if the results show the individual shareowner population is not down again.

In fact, some experts who follow investment trends closely, believe that the number of individual shareowners at present is no more than 15 million; in short, a 50 percent decline over the past decade.

This school of thought holds that so far as the division of market ownership is concerned, individuals have been net sellers of stock from 1960 onward and institutional investors have been net buyers. For example, data compiled recently by the Federal Reserve Board indicates that in the past eight years, individual shareowners have been net sellers of at least $40 billion worth of equities (including shares of mutual funds aside from those of the money-market variety.) Institutional holdings meanwhile have increased.

The one point on which almost everyone involved in the securities industry does agree is that the retail markets no longer are sellers' markets but buyers' markets—and in every sense of the term. As a result, relatively new concepts and expressions are now emerging on the sell side of the retail market. Among these are "marketing concept," "market research," and "financial planning."

The marketing concept first appeared as a new selling strategy in corporate America in the mid-1950s. Since then, it has reached full maturity and gained recognition as the most rewarding profit-producing mode in just about every industry except the securities industry. On Wall Street, marketing only now is beginning to win acceptance as the optimum strategy for improving bottom-line performance. It still has a long way to go before it gains full industry-wide adoption. Only a handful of firms have become marketing-conscious, and among these the firms with the biggest slices of the retail markets have made the most progress.

SELLERS' RESPONSES TO A BUYERS' MARKET

Responding to pressure from member firms, especially from those with the largest stakes in the retail market, the New York Stock Exchange initiated in 1977 a market research survey focused on small investors.

Market Assessment

The report, nationwide in scope and completed in 1978, found widespread preoccupation with "preserving" capital and purchasing power in order to keep abreast of inflation. The American public was deeply cautious about managing its money, placing it in areas where the smallest amount of risk was perceived (passbook savings, home ownership, other real estate, savings certificates, and life insurance). This discouraging report indicated that nearly 70 percent of those questioned were unwilling to accept more than the barest minimum of risk. Corporate stocks were viewed as entailing risk levels that they were unwilling to assume.

The deep concern all across the retail side of Wall Street prompted an analysis of the survey's findings with a view toward identifying problems perceived by clients or by potential clients. Competent and convincing responses were then assembled and offered to the member firms as a means of fostering positive action. Highlights of this professional evaluation are included below, particulary those having implications for career preparation.

Fostering Favorable Attitudes

In the area of fostering favorable public attitudes toward the securities industry, individual firms can help themselves and the industry by using the positive approach in their planning and public relations programs. Important areas for improved communication include moves involving timeliness and promptness in making buy-and-sell advices to customers, as well as tailoring and packaging investor services more accurately fitted to their needs and financial priorities.

Matching Services and Needs

More complete analysis of individual shareholders and potential shareholders can bring a better "match" between various kinds of publics and the investment products that are adapted to their needs. It is required that the account executive (A/E) be a "past master" at this. He must also be able to allay fears of risks in the securities market as compared with those in other financial markets. The appeal of "balanced risks" through use of a variety of brokerage products is uniquely the A/E's to foster as well.

Finding ways to expand the retail market among one-in-seven households planning to invest in equities for the first time, as well as among those present owners who plan to invest more actively, represents another area of challenge to the industry.

A Sizable Potential Market

Analysis of the survey revealed underutilized brokerage products needing attention. Most households having brokerage accounts are unfamiliar with the protection and benefits of margin accounts. Only 8 percent of some 45 million eligible households own or have owned corporate bonds; the remainder need to be made aware of the positive defensive attributes of bond ownership. Only one in twenty own municipals and less than one in thirty own shares in tax-free mutual funds.

Only one out of six public investors owns Keogh or IRA Plans, one out of ten has annuity plans, one out of sixteen has long-term U.S. bonds, and one out of twenty has U.S. Treasury bills and various convertibles. Such realities reveal a sizable retail market that can be successfully penetrated through educational programs and appropriate selling techniques. More recent studies may reveal significant movement into these areas of potential growth; however, the challenge is an abiding one.

Householder investor priorities revealed by the survey include more income for living expenses; family protection; combatting inflation; capital appreciation; tax minimization; and more income for retirement living. These all imply investment objectives stressing safety, stability, and good returns. The direction indicated for the retail arm of the investment community is that of devising marketing strategies and establishing selling tactics that bring together product-lines and services fully ad-dressing these identified needs. Also indicated is the necessity for continuing market research focused on the attitudes, motivations, needs and wants of U.S. households. This recognition is already manifest in the increase of market professionals now working full time as staff members of the Big 25 and at most of the major regional securities firms.

The realization that the retail investment market changed dramatically and perhaps, permanently, in the 1970's from a sellers' to a buyers' market has resulted in strenuous efforts on the part of the largest firms to tailor their expanded product lines to respond to the buyer's needs and wants. Their product lines now include real estate financing, employee relocation assistance, facilities for investing in precious metals, a much larger inventory of commodities, and services in assets management, financial counseling, and full financial planning designed to help households achieve their financial and investment goals.

EXPANDED CAREER OPPORTUNITIES

As securities firms add to their marketing efforts in response to buyer demands, broad new avenues of opportunities are opening to young people interested in pursuing careers in the securities industry. And if, as many industry spokesmen anticipate, double-digit inflation and interest rates return to more traditional levels and small investors participate again in the capital markets in larger numbers, the avenues of opportunity will become even broader.

Overleaf: Computer expert uses oscilloscope to check out wiring in a central processing unit. Technical positions have increased in response to massive reliance on computer technology in the securities industry. (Matar Studio Inc.)

CHAPTER 8

MODERN SECURITIES FIRMS

The securities industry is a whole composed of countless parts that come in many sizes, shapes, and descriptions. The Big 25 dominate news about Wall Street firms. To the individual investor in a community many miles removed from Manhattan, however, the small local firm handling her or his business is a much more important link to the investment world than the big nationwide firm that just opened a branch office down the street.

"Just opened a branch office" is what many of the giant firms have been doing as they have taken over the facilities of firms put out of business by the radical changes embodied in the Reform Act of 1975. In all, a hundred or more medium-sized and large firms have either closed their doors for good or have been absorbed by giant firms with sufficient capital, and more diversified earnings bases, that have enabled them to withstand the onslaught of five years of unrestricted competition in wide-open markets.

CHALLENGE FROM A NEW CORNER

This competition has involved more than head-to-head free-for-alls among the Big 25 battling to retain or increase their market shares of institutional business. Competition for retail business has emerged from a new corner: the discount house.

The big firms initially tended to discount the discount houses as not posing a serious threat to their retail business. But as the seventies ended, the small "executions only" houses were springing up like dandelions all over the investment landscape.

Since revenues from this way of doing business do not have to cover costs of research analysts, block traders, back office operations and the like, the discount firms can offer execution services at commission rates significantly below the rates charged by the giant all-purpose houses. The dollar differential offered by discount houses can be substantial. Piperack rates usually are a minimum of 50 percent below the commission prices of the all-purpose giants. Actual rates per transaction depend on the size of the individual investor's order. The following comparative table is typical:

No. of Shares Traded & Price	Full-Service Firm Rate	Typical Rate of Discount House	% Differential
400 Shs. @ $12	$118.00	58.40	51%
600 Shs. @ $15	173.00	74.00	57%
800 Shs. @ $25	310.00	120.00	61%
1,000 Shs. @ $30	416.00	140.00	66%

Estimates of how much discounting is going on in the retail markets vary from 5 percent to 15 percent of all shares traded. Some veteran observers expect discounting to become an increasingly serious competitive threat to the big retail firms.

"Three developments convince me that discounting is a serious business that is here to stay," a top executive at one of the largest retail houses said. He ticked the developments off: "First, there's a lot of undercover discounting going on right now among the big firms. If you have affluent retail customers of longstanding who ask for a knock-down in your published rates, they get it. Who gets how much of a knock-down will depend on how much trading volume the particular account generates, how long the account has been on the books, what other business relationships are involved between the account and our firm, and other considerations. A valued account looking for lower commission charges, however, usually gets them. How much lower can vary from one account to the next."

He continued, "The second development is that some of the big houses are in the process of setting up discount subsidiaries that will enable them to sell 'execution only' to those customers who are price-conscious about commission rates. That way, we may be able to hold on to that special type of customer and still sell the full package of retail services to our customers who want the whole bundle."

He added, "The third development I find unnerving is that the piperack houses are starting up their own trade association. Since this means they have to put up dues and other expenses to support their association, it also means they must be making a buck. And finally, it means they'll have a voice, through their association, in lobbying for legislative or regulatory changes affecting the securities business. Their interests won't necessarily coincide with ours."

It's obvious that the new discount firms, even speaking with one voice, will have only a whisper of influence compared to the giants, some of whom have a hundred or more branch offices, several thousands of employees, and multimillions of dollars in profits annually. As several experts have agreed, it's too early to tell whether the new smaller firms will have enough staying power if their limited financial resources are put to the test in a prolonged bear market.

The *Wall Street Journal,* in an article on January 4, 1980, dealing with the multiplication of new smaller firms, described this relationship between most small firms and the big all-purpose firms as follows:

"Scores of large and medium-sized houses did fold or were swallowed in mergers in the past few years, and *that* trend doesn't show any sign of abating. But the emphasis on competition in the 1975 securities legislation also made it relatively cheap and easy for a small firm to start up. And in 1976, the unfixing of the 'clearing' rates that small firms pay larger houses also helped the proliferation of new small-scale ventures.

Then the *Journal* added, "Most of the newly formed small firms provide individualized service and cheap rates that the bigger firms won't, don't or can't offer. But the key question is whether the new firms will have staying power to withstand the securities industry's traditional cycles and vicissitudes."

THE LARGE FIRMS: DIRECTIONS AND PATTERNS

While it seems likely that some smaller firms, in one form or another, will be able to carve a profitable existence out of securities in the future, it seems virtually certain that the very large firms will continue to dominate the industry. In the past decade or so, most of the largest Wall Street houses have been building their organizations along the same lines as the big industrial corporations.

Looking at the multibillion dollars' worth of annual sales and the multithousands of employees of the industrial corporations topping the *Fortune* 500 list, it's difficult to realize that these mammoths had modest beginnings. Note, however, that General Motors, General Electric, and General Foods started out as buck privates. They began as one-man ships or small partnerships that fused into companies. The companies then became privately-owned corporations, and finally publicly-owned corporations whose stocks are held by millions of investors.

The *Fortune* list of the Big 25 securities firms are moving in the same direction: 19 are incorporated, and of these 11 are publicly owned. Chances are, however, if the stock market ever returns to normal, and brokerage stocks begin trading near their book values, just about all of the largest sell side firms can be expected to pursue the additional capital available along the publicly-owned route.

Besides following the same ownership blueprints, the Big 25 have been developing much the same functional structures as the blue-chip industrials. The box-chart diagram that follows does not specifically apply to any one of the Big 25 but rather is a cross-sectional representation of how a typical modern firm may have its senior management responsibilities allocated and interlocked.

**Chairman
and
Chief Executive Officer**

Vice Chairman

- Corporate Finance and Underwriting
- Syndications
- Insurance
- Compliance
- Real Estate and Architecture

Vice Chairman

- Equity Transactions
- Floor Activities
- Research
- Institutional Sales
- International
- Mutual Funds
- Money Management

President

- Retail Sales and Branch Administration
- Marketing
- Advertising
- Public Relations
- Public Affairs

Executive Vice President

- Options
- Commodities
- Financial Instruments

Executive Vice President

- Administration
- Human Resources
- Operations

Executive Vice President

- Chief Financial Officer
- Treasurers Office
- Controllers Office

Executive Vice President

- Corporate Bonds
- Government Bonds
- Municipal Bonds
- Public Finance

Senior Vice President

- Legal
- General Counsel
- Corporate Secretary

First Vice President
- Internal Audit
- Management Reporting

The Big 25 usually have staffs of at least 1,000—and the very largest on up to 25,000. A representative firm among the Big 25, with a staff of 8,000 or so, could have a personnel profile that would look something like this:

Area	Number Employees
Head Office and Regional Headquarters	600
Retail Sales and Branch Administration	3,200
Institutional Sales and Trading (Equities)	150
Institutuional Sales and Trading (Fixed Income)	150
Equity Transactions (Exchanges, OTC, etc.)	200
Corporate Finance and Underwriting	200
Commodities, Options, Financial Instruments	100
Research	100
Operations (Back Office and Communications)	3,300
Total	8,000

The above functional grouping would be typical although it does not represent any specific sell side firm. It would include rank-and-file employees as well as those with top management official titles on down through the scores of vice presidents, assistant vice presidents, managers, and assistant managers. Officers (including A/Es) in the typical Big 25 firm usually are outnumbered by technicians, secretaries, statisticians, clerks and the like on a basis of about 20 to 1.

All the largest firms distinguish between their various staff members on the basis of "Exempt Positions" and "Non-Exempt Positions." The first classification consists of officers and supervisors with the highest salaries who are exempt from labor regulations requiring compensation for overtime work.

Those who are non-exempt receive time-and-a-half pay for work in excess of 40 hours per week, and double time for working on weekends and holidays.

The typical large firm may have as many as 300 individual job descriptions—senior management titles aside. A cross-section of such job descriptions might include:

Exempt Positions

Account Executive
Account Executive Training
  Manager
Accounting Manager
Compensation and Benefits
  Supervisor
Compliance Administrator
Computer-Based Systems Manager
Computer Operations Supervisor
Corporate Finance Officer
Corporate Bond Sales Manager
Data Processing Manager
Editor
Floor Broker (Stock Exchange)
Floor Broker (Commodities
  Exchange)
Government Bond Sales Manager
Government Agency Sales Manager
International Operations Manager
Institutional Sales Manager
Internal Auditing Manager
Money Management Director
Mutual Funds Manager
Operations Control Supervisor
Personnel Manager
Research Analyst
Research Librarian
Retirement Planning Manager
Syndicate Operations Supervisor
Systems Analyst
Trader, Blocks
Trader, Equities
Trader, Fixed-Income
Unit Trust Product Manager
Word Processing Systems
  Supervisor
Wire Services and Communications
  Manager

The above is only a sampling of the exempt positions in a large securities firm, as is the list below of the second category of job descriptions.

Non-Exempt Positions

Bank Loan Clerk
Bond Storage Clerk
Certificate Audit Clerk
Commodity Margin Clerk
Computer Operator
Data Processing Equipment
 Operator
Dividend Clerk
Editorial Assistant
Institutional Order Clerk
Inventory Control Clerk
Key Punch Operator
Library Assistant
Margin Clerk
Mutual Funds Clearance Clerk
Options Clerk
Options Clearance Clerk
Order Clerk
Personnel Clerk
Printer
Proxy Clerk
Purchase and Sale Clerk
Registration Assistant
Research Clerk
Secretary
Security Clearance Clerk
Security Control Clerk
Statistician
Stock Loan Clerk
Stock Record Clerk
Syndicate Clerk
Tape Librarian
Trading Clerk
Trade Adjustment Clerk
Transfer Clerk
Typist
Teletype Operator
Word Processing System Clerk

The above cross-sectional lists of job titles at typical full-service securities firms only hint at the massive changes in sell side houses during the past dozen years or so. From the late sixties onward, Wall Street has been moving swiftly to close the "big business gap" between itself and industrial corporate America.

NEW DEVELOPMENTS AS CHANGE FACTORS

A huge variety of new career opportunities in the securities industry opened in the past decade or so, and will continue to open in the eighties, as the result of these four basic factors that have dramatically changed the big investment firms: (1) The advent of the corporate structure; (2) increased automation and computerization; (3) broad diversification of product lines; and (4) the need for sophisticated human resources: planning, recruitment, and training. Each of these will be discussed in turn.

Impact of the Corporate Structure

As indicated earlier, the shift from closely-held partnerships to publicly-held corporations has resulted in pervasive changes in the organizational and functional structures of securities firms. New career opportunities have been created, or have evolved, simply as the result of incorporation and the added functions that that entails.

Incorporation has changed management functions up and down the ladder. Combined with the tidal wave of mergers, incorporation has increased, and hugely, the size of Wall Street organizations. As a firm increases in its spread and in its staff, there is a growing need for unified and effective management within multiple areas.

No longer is it possible for a handful of partners to maintain control over all parts of their organization. Rather, senior management must rely on competent middle and lower management to assure effective day-to-day functioning. This means not only a greater number of managerial personnel, but also the development of more specialized managers and assigning them more authority and autonomy. Continual growth has made it impossible for the senior management of a corporation with five, eight, ten, (or more) thousands of employees to have intimate knowledge of both the people and their activities on the job. Similarly, a manager in the operations division cannot have day-to-day awareness of what may be happening in the corporate finance or human resources divisions other than to the extent that what may be happening has direct impact on his own area of responsibility.

Of course government regulation is not new to securities firms, especially since the creation of the SEC in the thirties. However, government regulation as it affects firms as corporations *is* comparatively new. It has created positions that previously didn't exist. These include, among others:

- Equal Employment Opportunity administrators to assure that the corporation is conforming to EEOC guidelines.
- Employee benefits administrators to assure compliance with ERISA regulations.
- Informed management personnel to assure that the firm is conforming with all the numerous and different financial reporting requirements of various government and regulatory bodies.

As with any large corporation, the sheer volume of information that must be handled, processed, disseminated, and comprehended has expanded enormously. The result here also is new opportunities: communications analysts, data processors of all descriptions, a wide variety of technicians and technical specialists, editors, writers, and systems analysts for expediting the flow of both manually-controlled and, increasingly, computer-controlled information and data.

Impact of Automation and Computerization

The huge increase in transactional volume, plus the vast increase in the size of securities firms, have created industry-wide needs to process efficiently mountains of data and information.

In the late sixties, for example, when the volume of trading reached 15 or 16 million shares daily on the Big Board (matched by similar increases in other securities markets), the securities industry was virtually paralyzed by this incessant expansion in service demands.

Currently, trading volume on the New York Stock Exchange averages 35 million shares daily. And a number of days when volume has been much greater have not triggered any of the panic or avalanche of "fails" of a decade earlier. This is because the securities industry, as do almost all other industries, now places heavy reliance on computer-centered data processing systems. Today's margin clerks use computer printouts to verify the accuracy of margin accounts—in contrast to the former manual notations on the margins of client account records.

As the securities industry was rather surprised to discover after a recent survey of its clients' primary interests in the industry's services, "accurate and timely reporting of account status" was identified overwhelmingly as the most important service expected of securities firms. Not good stock picks, or fast option executions, or in-depth financial planning, but accurate and timely reporting of a client's account status.

The efficient handling of the massive amounts of information, which must be processed daily to keep client accounts updated, alone would be totally impossible without the computer. Nor could the computer even begin to do its job without programmers, without data processing specialists, without keypunch operators, and input/output clerks.

The range of career opportunities in electronic data processing (commonly referred to as EDP) and in information systems analysis and design are as full and varied in the securities industry as in any other major industry. These are the foremost areas of potential career fulfillment since they are the most rapidly growing in the entire industry.

As large corporations, full-service securities firms rely on EDP not only for client account information but also for internal payroll and other personnel requirements.

Computers also are used extensively for portfolio analysis, for technical research analysis, and for financial planning, the latter in behalf both of the clients' interests and the interests of the securities firm itself. Top management, with the aid of computer specialists, can now project much more realistic growth and profit goals than through the "by guess and by golly" intuitive decisions of the not-so-distant yesterdays.

Judgmental decisions based on the "seat of the pants" are acceptable when the wearer of the pants alone is affected by the outcome. But top management of a worldwide corporation, with many thousands of employees and hundreds of thousands of customers, needs all the help it can get, electronic and otherwise, in making its business development and profit-producing decisions.

As the chief executive of one of the largest securities firms has commented, "In the fifties and early sixties, this job was a cinch. In the late sixties it began to get much more complicated. In the seventies, it became downright dangerous."

Impact of Product Diversification

Since the sixties, but especially in the past few years, diversification has been the name of the game in the securities industry. Depending on how it defines its "product line," the modern securities firm of any size will have well over 100 separate products (read here "services") to market.

The percentage of total revenues attributable to traditional equity business has been shrinking for most large firms while revenues from other products has been increasing. The traditionally breath-taking soaring and plunging of the stock market becomes much more tolerable when other stable sources of revenues—and profits—are available.

Product diversification obviously has had a major impact on career opportunities in the marketing strategies and sales functioning of the big Wall Street houses. Full scale acceptance of the importance of marketing as a concept has yet to be achieved by most large firms. However, it is gaining ground. Increasingly, the biggest firms also are awakening to the need, too, for marketing specialists in such products as tax-advantaged investments, financial planning and retirement planning, and insurance and real estate investment products.

No one individual, no matter how experienced in marketing planning and implementation, can be expected to have a complete grasp on each of the products in the multiple product lines now offered by the major sell side firms. Thus the need has evolved for marketing specialists as well as overall market strategy-makers.

Nor can any account executive (commonly called an A/E)—no matter how gray his beard is or how magic are his selling capabilities—be expected to be fully conversant in every aspect of all the possible investment alternatives now available to his clients. The most successful A/Es in modern securities firms are those who know where their firm's specialists are and how to use them—commodities specialists, options specialists, financial planning specialists, and retirement planning specialists.

Training programs no longer are one-time or spasmodic efforts. Among the most profitable of the largest firms, they are conducted as on-going efforts that affect all the people involved either directly in selling—as the A/Es—or indirectly as those providing support to the sales force. Such training programs (and the smartest top managements make sure they, too, are involved) include audio-visual as well as written programs. Since training programs are only as effective as their intrinsic quality, most of the largest firms are at least beginning to recognize their urgent need for *professional* writers and editors as well as qualified professionals in producing audio/video tapes for training and marketing purposes.

Human Resources

It used to be called "Personnel."

In the old partnership days, the partner in charge of people at the sell side firm usually was in charge of back office operations as well. Among many firms, expanding or cutting the back office clerical staff was the easiest and most expeditious way of controlling expenses.

What happens if the stock market volume goes up 20 percent? Hire 20 percent more people. Volume down 20 percent? Pink slips accordingly.

Last-in-first-out inventory control of personnel was the rule-of-thumb, although not a hard and fast rule. If one of the partners had a nephew learning the business by putting in a temporary stint shuffling back office paper, the nephew would have permanent working papers, regardless of trading volume.

Reporting to the partner in charge of operations would be a "Personnel Manager." His primary responsibilities included maintaining a productive rapport with employment agencies, keeping employee records, and getting payroll checks out on time to the right employees in the right amounts.

What about employee benefit programs? There was a bonus check at the end of the year for those with sufficient time on the job—and assuming it had been a good year. A year was "good" when the partners decided it was good.

A very good year often meant a very good bonus check—but not always. Maybe one of the senior partners with a big chunk of capital in the firm had decided to pack up and go soak up some sun on a vacation. Then, off went the partner, out went the capital, and down went the bonus pool.

The New Approach: Human Resources

The old days, inevitably and thankfully, have gone forever. Symbolic of the radical changes in the attitudes and policies of modern securities firms is the common use of "Human Resources" as the term for managing the firm's people-needs.

It took longer, it's true, for Wall Street to get *The Message* than the rest of corporate America. But *The Message* (here referring to the central operating concept) has been received, loud and clear.

The Message (Part I) says: There are only three kinds of resources available to any profit-making enterprise: human resources, raw material resources, and financial resources. *The Message (Part II)* says: In the long run, and often in the short run, too, the success of any competitive enterprise will depend 99.99 percent on the quality of its human resources.

This applies "in spades" to the securities industry since it is first and foremost a people-to-people business. It is especially applicable to the service sector.

Large securities firms now are as fully aware as other large organizations of their endless need for competent people. Human resource functions have become structured and specialized in the big Wall Street houses. For example, a large firm that wants to attract and keep competent people must have a competitive compensation program—one that can compete successfully with other securities firms and also with large organizations in other industries.

A workable program must have compensation managers and analysts who can evaluate a long list of positions, exempt and non-exempt, and assure that salaries and benefits are competitive up and down the line. Equal employment regulations prescribe equitable hiring and compensation policies.

Advances for Minorities and Women

"Equal employment opportunities" in the case of securities firms means a concerted, intensified effort to provide women, as well as ethnic minority groups, with higher-paying, more satisfying jobs. Wall Street some time ago removed barriers to the advancement of ethnic minorities. Only lately, however, have women begun to get the recognition and status that is their fundamental right.

The lesser role of women on Wall Street has been in evidence at other management levels as well as at the very top. Women hold roughly about one-third of all the jobs in securities firms. Only 7 percent are in management positions, as compared to not quite 20 percent in all industries nationwide, according to U.S. Department of Labor surveys.

The functional structure of women on Wall Street traditionally was that of a pyramid. The greatest number of women would work at the base of the pyramid as clerks and secretaries. Moving up the pyramid, the level of pay would rise but the number of women would decrease. At higher levels would be the stockbrokers (also known as registered representatives and account executives regardless of their sex).

Knowing someone already with a securities firm remains an excellent door-opener. Once inside, performance and merit are the chief criteria for advancement—for women and men alike. This requires special skills in job evaluation and performance of employees on one hand, and careful monitoring of the firm's employment practices and policies on the other.

In addition to the paycheck, employees at all levels are vitally interested in opportunities for growth and personal development. This calls for broad-based employee enrichment programs, including management development from within. Thus another specialized need: people who can plan and implement training programs for literally thousands of women and men comprising a large securities firm's nationwide staff.

THE ACCOUNT EXECUTIVE

The most widespread human resources in the typical large securities firm is the A/E. The A/E is the firm's chief point of contact with its customers—indeed for millions of investors the registered representative may be the only point of contact.

"Registered" means the A/E (or "stockbroker") has been accredited by the New York Stock Exchange or National Association of Securities Dealers. Following training periods and after passing mandatory examinations, the representative is registered with government regulatory agencies as a man or woman qualified to provide investment services to the public. Modern securities firms spare no effort in their A/E recruitment programs to get candidates with high integrity and an ability to relate to people.

But there are additional criteria as well, as indicated by these guidelines of one major firm:

ACCOUNT EXECUTIVE SELECTION CRITERIA

Confidence and Persuasiveness in the Face of Rejection. The A/E maintains solid confidence despite obstacles and reversals. The A/E must be clear and convincing, hitting home with persuasive ideas that stimulate sales.

Self-discipline in Work. The A/E must prepare, schedule, and execute her or his activities with little direction or supervision. To accomplish this in the face of predictable and unpredictable demands of the job, the A/E must plan and manage her or his time efficiently.

Use of Available Materials to Generate Sales in a Responsible Way. From materials provided, the A/E must recognize those ideas that match a client's needs. Despite the desire for income, the A/E does not push a recommendation that is inappropriate for the customer's needs and objectives.

Accurate Appraisal of Oneself and One's Understanding of Others. The A/E is open to the possibility of being wrong. To minimize this possibility, the A/E listens alertly and requests verification that the client has been accurately understood. The A/Es periodically evaluate their own performance in order to become more effective.

Responsible Pursuit of Organizational Policies and Image. The A/E must represent the Company in a professional manner in all customer dealings. The A/E must comply with company and regulatory procedures and policies. Promptness, dependability, and trust-worthiness are essential for effective customer service.

Performance of a Variety of Tasks Quickly and Accurately. The A/E must deal with numerical information and verbal instruction in an effective manner. Because of the immense time pressures associated with the job, a variety of demands must be handled simultaneously and with great speed. However, despite the need for speed in a distracting environment, the A/E must maintain a high level of accuracy in arithmetic calculations and in the understanding of new service requests.

Social Adeptness. The A/E must develop good relations with the variety of people that make up her or his clientele, and maintain those relations across varied market conditions. The successful A/E is an aggressive salesperson who can, nonetheless, maintain good rapport with clients.

Effectively Delivered Presentations. The A/E must be able to plan the presentation for maximum effectiveness. He or she must be organized, comfortable, and articulate when speaking to an audience.

Ability to Act in the Face of Uncertainty. The A/E operates under uncertain market conditions. This uncertainty cannot freeze the A/E into inaction. Rather, the A/E must be able to consider whatever information is available, although that information may be far from complete, and make a firm decision. While avoiding blind chances, the A/E must take confident action based on calculated risks.

Besides meeting recruitment criteria such as the above, women and men interested in becoming stockbrokers—and those who prove to be most successful at it—are those with a fundamental interest in business, economics, and the securities markets: what they are and how they work.

In recruiting A/E candidates externally, educational requirements vary from one firm to the next. Some require college degrees; others look for graduate school training. Still others, put a premium on prior experience in another business in the belief that such experience will assure a more objective evaluation of investment gaols and opportunities.

An increasing number of the large firms are making a special effort to encourage the professional development of people already on staff to a point where they can qualify as A/E candidates. Such employees usually can take six credits per term at an accredited school or institution and, upon satisfactory completion of the courses, are reimbursed for the entire course tuition.

Intensive Training Leading to Registration

A/E candidates undergo an intensive training program preliminary to "registration." Typically, a training program lasts five months. A breakdown of probable experiences would look like this:

Nine weeks: Securities Basic Study Course (SBSC)
Two weeks: Prepare for General Securities Examination
One day: Take the General Securities Examination
Five weeks: Special in-branch training
Five weeks: Head office training and wrap-up

The various examinations probe the prospective A/E's full body of knowledge relating to securities markets operations, brokerage office procedures, characteristics of investment vehicles, investment banking and other aspects of corporate finance, techniques for analyzing corporate earnings performance and potential, economic forecasting, tax consequences of securities transactions. Other subjects include payout procedures in corporate liquidation, tax consequences of alternate methods of figuring depreciation, shorthand of stock order quotations, and the workings of specific federal regulations.

The stockbroker's sense of achievement on receiving written notice of completion of registration requirements matches the thrill of being awarded a diploma for successfully completing even longer periods of formal education. The certificate of registration means one is eligible for employment by almost all firms in the securities industry—on both the buy and sell sides of the capital markets. Many of the major institutional investors now require that their non-clerical employees pass the General Securities Examination. Most institutions will underwrite the costs of attending the special schools that offer the necessary courses.

"Stockbrokers are always in school," a senior vice president at one of the major brokerage firms said recently. "Years ago, the broker's product line remained fairly constant—stocks, bonds, or convertibles. Now it seems that every week something new is coming down the pike—and if our people can't discuss it intelligently with our customers, they lose confidence in us. Confidence and trust are the prerequisites of this business."

Confidence *and* trust—are they not the same thing?

"No, although they may seem to be," the senior v.p. said. "If you know a tight-rope walker has pushed a wheel-barrow across Niagara Falls, you can be reasonably confident that he can do it again. If you trust him, you get into the wheel-barrow."

He added, "People who trust their stockbrokers largely will be guided by the investment advice they get from them."

Warrants, life insurance, tax-shelter and retirement plans, government and municipal securities, commodities and financial futures, as well as listed and unlisted stocks, bonds, options, and an increasing variety of mutual funds—stockbrokers have to be familiar with all such products in order to help a customer put together an optimum package of such vehicles suitable to the customer's specific investment objectives.

Stockbrokers also are expected to keep abreast of developments in Wall Street's most precious commodity: news. As a group, the 50,000 or so brokers in the U.S. probably are the most accomplished speed-readers in the business world. They have to be. Besides keeping up with their own firm's unending flow of research reports, they have to at least skim through a number of the more influential business and financial publications—The *Wall Street Journal, Fortune, Forbes, Business Week,* and often the *Harvard Business Review,* among many others.

Aware that economic and political events are inextricably intertwined, as has been fully demonstrated since the OPEC oil embrago in 1973, stockbrokers also have to keep on top of the general news. They read the *New York Times,* or the *Washington Post,* or the *Los Angeles Times,* or the *Chicago Sun Times,* or the *Dallas Post,* or the *Boston Globe,* or any combination of these or other general news publications.

CONCLUDING NOTES ON A/E COMPENSATION

Is it all worthwhile?

Financially, it can be very worthwhile. Account executive compensation depends to a great degree on the stockbroker's own efforts. While compensation may vary somewhat from one firm to the next, the bottom line includes attractive pay-out rates dictated by the type and size of transactions completed, as well as scheduled bonus amounts that vary with gross receipts. Some A/Es make as much each year as the chief executives of their firms, meaning upwards of $300,000 including bonuses. Others, and most others, net much less. Those just starting out do well to top $20,000. Based on Security Industry Association studies, the average A/E in 1979 earned approximately $34,000, up from not quite $30,000 in 1978 owing largely to higher trading volume.

Other compensation rates also were increasing commensurately throughout the industry. For example, a trade publication in January 1980, reported that one of the largest Wall Street firms had increased, effective the first pay period of the new year, across-the-board pay increases of 8 percent for its lower salaried employees (those earning less than $12,000 annually) and an increase of 5 percent for those earning from $12,000 to $20,000. These increases were for base annual compensation, meaning they were aside from individual merit increases resulting from periodic salary reviews. Nor did they include additional compensation in the form of employee benefits, now equivalent to about 25¢ to 35¢ for each base compensation dollar.

Overleaf: Traders carry orders received from clients or act as specialists concerned with price movements of particular stocks. (Matar Studio Inc.)

CHAPTER 9

MARKETPLACES AND MARKETMAKERS

NEEDED: A NATIONAL MARKET SYSTEM

The U.S. securities industry has been built on two types of marketplaces—auction markets and over-the-counter markets—and two kinds of marketmakers—agencies and dealers. Although each of these elements is separately identifiable, in the overall functions of the securities markets they have been connected—loosely connected, it's true, but connected nonetheless.

In the two centuries of the nation's independent existence, these markets have been able to perform their essential function: capital formation to support the U.S. expanding economy. As dramatically demonstrated in the past two decades, however, the securities markets have not been able to perform well enough. They have not been able to provide sufficient amounts of the right kind of capital to support the stable growth of the United States economy, and thus help to affirm the leadership role of this country in the global community of free industrialized nations.

This failure is not attributable solely to inadequate and inefficient methods of capital formation. It has been a human failure in both the government sector and the private sector of the U.S. economy—a failure to identify our national priorities and to plan and control the use of our human resources, raw material resources *and* financial resources accordingly.

Our capital markets clearly have been inadequately structured and inefficiently operated. Five years ago the Securities Reform Act (more commonly referred to as the 1975 Act) was passed by Congress to enable legislation to weld our loosely connected capital markets into an efficient national market system.

Some progress has been made towards this goal; however, there is a great deal of distance still to go. Whether this goal will ever be reached, only time will tell. That time well may be the decade of the 1980s.

ROLE OF THE EXCHANGES

Auction Markets: The New York Stock Exchange. It is not the marketplace where the largest volume of securities is traded; the government bond market is larger. Nor is it "the center of the financial markets" as many of its members have proclaimed; more objective observers reserve that distinction for the Federal Reserve.

But there can be little doubt that the New York Stock Exchange is the best known, and most influential, securities marketplace in existence. Overall, and over the long term, what happens on the Big Board gets more public attention than perhaps all other parts of the investment markets combined.

Similarly, any time when the general subject of securities trading is discussed, the chief focal point will be the New York Stock Exchange. This is true even though the importance of equities in the galaxy of securities has been diminishing rather than increasing in recent years.

Of course everything is relative—including such statements as the importance of equities is diminishing. Certainly any of the 600 or so Exchange employees on the trading floor of the Big

Board would have challenged that statement on that historic day in October 1979, when trading volume reached 82 million shares. Only fourteen months earlier, August 3, 1978, daily volume of 66 million shares had set a new record that spokesmen at the Exchange expected to last "at least for a few years."

More than 7.2 billion shares were traded in 1978, over a third more than the previous record of 5.4 billion in 1976.

The tremendous surge in volume continued in 1979 for the year as a whole: a new record high of 8.1 billion shares. Daily average trading topped 35 million shares compared with 29 million in 1978 and 21 million in 1977.

Overall Workings of the Big Board. Obviously, the Exchange works, and it works fairly well at what it does: a marketplace where a huge volume of shares can be traded. Let's see what goes on at 11 Wall Street, headquarters for the biggest auction market in the world.

First, a few of the things the Exchange does *not* do: It does not issue the securities traded through its facilities. It neither buys or sells these securities. It does not set the prices on these securities. The Exchange provides the marketplace where securities are bought and sold. The Big Board is a not-for-profit corporation owned by the 1,366 individuals who have bought seats on the Exchange and who work for securities firms known as member organizations.

The number of seats remains fairly constant, 1,366 since 1953. You can buy one only from someone who already owns one, and the prices of seats are anything but constant. In the 20th century, for example, the highest price was $515,000 in late 1968–early 1969 and the lowest price $17,000 in 1942 during World War II.

The approximately 500 member organizations of the Exchange are profit-making companies, of course, although the percentage of their profits originating as commission revenues from Exchange transactions has been diminishing, especially for the largest securities houses. The chief reason for this has been the shrinkage in profit margins derived from institutional trading commissions. The 1975 Act let a competitive tiger out of the cage that has virtually shredded institutional trading profit margins. Member organizations earnestly have been developing other sources of revenues to replace the pre-1975 fat commissions from institutional transactions. As the securities markets have become increasingly institutionalized in the past five years, competition for the order flow from institutions has further intensified and profits directly derived from this source have become pathetically anemic.

While profit margins have remained comparatively steady in retail trading, the volume of these orders has diminished significantly as a percentage of Exchange turnover. An estimated 75 percent of the Big Board's daily volume consists of institutional orders. About 15 percent consists of retail orders, and the remaining 10 percent reflects transactions for the member organizations' own accounts.

In other words, by far the greatest volume of trading on the Exchange reflects agency business, i.e., member firms buying or selling shares in behalf of their customers. These transactions take place at the 22 posts where some 2,000 corporate equities listed on the Exchange are traded.

Varieties of Brokers. Looking down at the Exchange floor from the visitor's gallery during a busy trading session, it takes a trained eye to distinguish the several varieties of stockbrokers heeling-and-toeing it around the floor. Most of the fast walkers (running is not permitted) are stockbrokers responding to orders received from the sales forces of their firms. These orders can originate from A/Es in branch offices as far away as Hawaii or from institutional sales people at a member firm's head office nearby in the financial district of Manhattan.

Other stockbrokers in motion on the floor may be registered competitive marketmakers (RCM), a new category of Exchange member as of May 1, 1978. The RCM has both affirmative and negative obligations to maintain a fair and orderly market in the open bidding at a trading post for a stock. This person is expected to make a bid or offer if asked by a floor official or by a floor broker holding an unexecuted customer's order. The RCM functions chiefly as a dealer. In effect, the RCM both competes with and supplements the role of the specialist.

The specialist is assigned a group of listed stocks at a designated trading post. He or she has the dual responsibility of maintaining an orderly market in the assigned stocks and of executing the limit orders left with her or him by floor brokers of other member organizations.

The specialists have three characteristics that distinguish them from other stockbrokers on the floor: they are not movers, but remain fixed at their assigned post; they act as both agent and dealer in maintaining an orderly market in their stocks; they have the best inside view of anyone on the Exchange when inordinate buying or selling trading pressures begin to build.

An orderly market exists when the price movements of a stock have reasonable continuity and depth. This is usually accomplished by the stockbrokers on the floor who comprise the "crowd" in front of the trading posts. They execute the buy and sell orders of their customers about 80 percent of the time without the intervention of the specialist.

The specialists step in to avoid the development of large price gaps or large price fluctuations in their assigned stocks. Whenever there is a temporary imbalance or absence of public supply or demand, the specialists insert their own bids or offers. In this role, they act as dealers, meaning they are trading for their own account.

They act as agents when they execute limit orders to buy or sell at prices either significantly above or below the current market price. These orders, left with them by other floor brokers, are logged in their books. The specialists keep a separate book for each of the stocks under their jurisdiction.

There are some sixty specialist firms, and not quite 400 individual specialists, on the Exchange. The institutionalization of the stock market has diminished the role of the specialist since the big institutions often submit block orders consisting of thousands of shares. The dollars involved in such transactions ofteen exceed the financial capacity of a specialist. When this happens, block orders often are transacted "upstairs" by "position houses." These are some of the largest firms that use their own capital to inventory sizable amounts of the 200 or 300 stocks most actively traded.

Among the 2,500 bonds listed on the Big Board, only about one-third are traded on the average day and just about all large orders are executed away from the Exchange. Bond traders at the Exchange are referred to by stockbrokers as "the bond crowd" and bond transactions take place in an area away from the main floor.

Subsidiary Organizations. The New York Stock Exchange, as well as most other securities marketplaces, relies on several affiliated and subsidiary organizations in providing investment services. Chief among these, at least from the investor's viewpoint, is the Securities Investor Protection Corporation (SIPC).

The SIPC is an outgrowth of a trust fund the Big Board used to maintain in behalf principally of its member organizations. Its purpose was to provide financial help in order to avoid the embarassment of bankruptcy resulting from a firm's failure. Congress has passed the Securities Investor Protection Act, making it mandatory to provide at least nominal protection for John and Jane Doe in the event a firm has to be liquidated. Funds for the SIPC are derived from organizations in the securities industry. It is not a government agency but a non-profit membership corporation. Protection is limited to $100,000 per customer account of which a maximum of $40,000 can be used for cash claims.

Another subsidiary service organization is the National Security

Clearing Corporation (the NSCC). This is a refinement and expansion of a former wholly-owned clearing subsidiary of the Big Board. Three years ago the Exchange merged its clearing operations with those of the American Stock Exchange to form the NSCC, jointly owned by both exchanges and separately managed and guided by an independent board of directors. Also separately managed with an independent board of directors is the Depository Trust Company, a central depository for securities certificates designed to eliminate the scurrying back and forth of messengers delivering certificates from old to new owners as the result of trading. Ownership of the DTC includes not only the member organizations comprising the major marketplaces but also a sizable number of large institutional investors.

In 1972, the Big Board and the American Stock Exchange joined forces to form the Securities Industry Automation Corporation (SIAC), with the NYSE two-thirds owner and the Amex one-third. The motivation for this union was the "fails" massacre during the 1968–1970 crisis. The SIAC provides clearing, electronic data processing, communications, and systems development services to its owners and their affiliates for which they are charged the costs designated for such services.

Auction Markets: The American Stock Exchange

The second largest stock exchange, widely referred to as the Amex by the present generation, always has been regarded as a much more colorful and adventurous marketplace than the much bigger and more prestigious exchange on the other side of Trinity Church graveyard.

Chris Welles, in his excellent book, *The Last Days of the Club*, describes the origins of the ASE as follows:

> "The Amex evolved from a floating marketplace of milling, shouting individuals collectively known as 'the Curb' because they sprawled over several street

curbs in the Wall Street area. Frequented mostly by rather raffish brokers unable to gain admittance to the NYSE, the Curb specialized in small issues considered too speculative by the well-bred gentlemen of the Exchange, who sported silk hats and swallowtail coats during business hours... Gradually, a kind of symbiotic relationship between the two markets evolved. In an arrangement which persists to this day, a new and untested issue would be traded first on the Curb; when it became seasoned, it would move to the more prestigious senior exchange, whereupon the Curb would stop trading it."

Gradually, the membership of the Curb changed in character, particularly after it constructed its own building and formally became the American Stock Exchange. Currently, about 90 percent of Amex members are NYSE members as well. Although it has a separate management and board of directors, the by-laws and regulations of the Amex are closely structured along the lines of those of the Big Board.

In recent years, however, the Amex has become a much more independent marketplace. One reason has been its explosive growth in volume. For example, at the beginning of 1978, the number of shares traded on the Big Board outnumbered the Amex by about 10 to 1. By the end of the year this was down to 5 to 1. In 1979, share volume on the Amex was almost 1 billion and was expected to pass this milestone in 1980.

Even more spectacular growth has taken place in options. While the Big Board was emulating Hamlet in its efforts to decide whether or not it should be in the options market, the Amex jumped in with both feet in 1975. That year it traded 3.5 million contracts. In 1978, the total was 14.4 million and in 1979, 17.4 million.

While the Amex was averaging 70,000 option contracts daily in 1979, the NYSE was still on the side-lines. The Big Board has notified the SEC it would like to get into this highly profitable business, but it seems unlikely that it will become a major factor much before 1981. Meanwhile, the Big Board's frustration has mounted as the Chicago Board of Options Exchange and the Amex have been making hay as the principal options marketplaces for shares listed on the New York Stock Exchange.

Auction Markets: The Regional Exchanges

Aside from the two largest stock marketplaces in New York, at one time there were fifteen other marketplaces in major commercial and financial centers. Moreover, the consolidation among securities firms during the sixties and seventies has been accompanied by a similar contraction in the number of regional exchanges.

For example, the Philadelphia-Baltimore-Washington stock markets have united their organizations into the Philadelphia Stock Exchange. The Chicago stock exchange became the keystone for the Midwest Stock Exchange which has combined several additional regional exchanges under that flag.

Before the consolidation wave, most of the regional exchanges were regarded as relatively insignificant factors in the auction markets. But with the development of the composite tape and highly sophisticated communications and electronic data processing systems, the regional exchanges have become important cogs in securities trading.

Aside from the members who own seats on these regional exchanges, there are thousands of employees working in a broad variety of occupations at these marketplaces. The staffs of these exchanges—and they are continually expanding—include lawyers, economists, a vast array of computer and electronic data processing operators and technicians, communication systems designers, and the supplementary force of statisticians, secretaries, and clerks.

ROLE OF THE OVER-THE-COUNTER MARKETS

In several respects, the OTC market is a market of superlatives: it is the oldest, largest, most heterogeneous, and most innovative securities market in the nation. It never was nor is it today a physical location like the buildings that house the various stock exchanges. Rather it is a communications network consisting of about 4,000 broker-dealer firms blanketing the nation. These firms range from two or three person operations to the giant supermarkets on the Big 25 list.

Being a network, rather than a place, the OTC handles securities transactions on the negotiated-trading principle, as opposed to the auction method used in the exchanges. From early on, government operations and businessmen's debt issues were financed by securities traded over the counters of private banking organizations.

Evolution of OTC Trading

The evolution of OTC trading, from its primitive origins to its present stature as a nationwide market-network, can be summarized as three development phases.

Phase I covers roughly the eighteenth and nineteenth centuries. Initially, OTC transactions consisted largely of small trades handled by small firms, transactions that were very local in character because of the lack of communications facilities. However, with the advent of the telegraph and telephone in the latter half of the nineteenth century, and the general heightening of the public's interest in investments as a reservoir for savings, OTC trading grew rapidly. This is when it became widely known as over-the-counter securities trading.

In Phase II, the first half of this century, the expanding securities industry extended its reach from border-to-border and coast-to-coast. Since entry into the industry was easiest through the OTC door, trading in unlisted stocks attracted thousands of novices. Many securities salespeople got their start as part-time employees, and their marketing efforts frequently were far afield from the presumed disciplined and controlled sales efforts of the stockbrokers representing the member firms of the exchanges.

Phase III, covering the current era, has been a truly phenomenal development stage for the OTC market.

Just as the exchanges came under more and more regulation, so did the OTC. A major piece of legislation affecting the OTC market was the Securities Acts Amendments of 1964. The effect was to change the diffuse and sprawling OTC market into a more tightly regulated marketplace. The supervision and control of the OTC broker-dealers was centered much more effectively in the National Association of Securities Dealers (NASD) under the overall supervision of the SEC. Sales personnel in OTC broker-dealer firms were required to pass the same General Securities Examination as applied to registered representatives of exchange member firms. Member firm officers were required to pass the principal's examination as well.

The widespread diversity of the OTC market is reflected in the great variety of its constituent firms as well as in the variety of securities traded. Uncle Sam, by far the largest issuer of securities, trades his vast array of government bonds, notes, and certificates in the OTC market. So does Uncle Fred, the owner of a small company that goes public by issuing several thousand shares for sale to investors for the first time. In fact, with a very few exceptions, all corporations that sell their equities to the public for the first time do so via the OTC market.

Between Uncle Sam and Uncle Fred, OTC issuers come in all sizes and from every corner of the nation. They include states, municipalities, and other local government entities; they include the great majority of insurance companies and banks, most of the utility companies, mutual funds, money market funds, investment companies, and variable annuity underwriters.

Workings of the OTC Market

OTC firms function both as brokers, or middle-man agencies, and as dealers (buying or selling for their own accounts) in serving millions of investors. However, the greatest volume of transactions is handled by firms acting as dealers.

The fundamental difference between trading OTC and on the exchanges is illustrated in this example: The stockbroker with a routine order to buy a Big Board listed stock simply goes to the appropriate post and, assuming the order is "at the market," gets the best price available in the crowd at the post. Under the auction process, he or she has at best only two other alternatives: the specialist acting as a dealer, or a registered marketmaker.

On the other hand, an OTC broker-dealer, acting as either an agent or a principal, usually can test a much larger number of marketmakers to determine their bid-and-asked quotations on an OTC stock. In doing so, the broker-dealer does not have to disclose whether he or she represents a buying (bid) or selling (asked) interest in the particular security.

On most exchanges, only one specialist makes a market in listed stocks; in the OTC situation, however, there may be a half-dozen or more dealers competing in a particular security. Therefore, broker-dealers have much broader opportunities to negotiate the best price for their customers and themselves, especially in the larger OTC issues.

Competition, historically the catalyst of destruction for Big Board members of the Club, in practice is the great boom for investors in OTC securities. Individuals can shop around among a number of OTC dealers to get the lowest transaction charge. However, the commission rates for trading listed issues are fixed (except for the discounting described earlier) in the auction (or exchange) markets.

Innovations by NASD in the OTC Market

By 1971, under the leadership of the NASD, the OTC market had grown from a diffuse trading mixture of brokers and dealers relying upon telephone and teletype communications into a cohesive nationwide market system. This miracle of transformation was made possible by the introduction in early 1971 of the National Association of Securities Dealers Automated Quotation System, commonly called NASDAQ, a computer-centered quotation system that gave the OTC market instant nationwide visibility.

The NASDAQ system is an electronic link between almost all major retail firms and OTC marketmakers. On specially designed television-type display units, a broker-dealer can press a few buttons and get, instantaneously, bid and asked prices, listed in order of the most favorable being offered by OTC marketmakers. Thus, NASDAQ dealers can quickly identify the best market for customer orders and can negotiate trades with appropriate marketmakers.

The immediacy of such trading contrasts with transactions on an exchange when limit orders often must be held until buy-and-sell prices can be matched or until the specialist buys or sells for her or his own account.

A GAME OF KEEP-UP

The introduction of NASDAQ encouraged the New York stock exchanges into adopting composite tapes, the electronic quotation systems whereby the trades in their respective listed stocks are reported wherever they take place in the auction markets. Selected regionally listed stocks, which substantially meet the listing requirements of the New York exchanges, are also carried on the composite tapes. Additionally, subscribers can obtain last sale information by questioning the composite quotation systems.

Hardly had the New York exchanges finished congratulating themselves for at least partly closing the technological gap opened by NASDAQ, when NASD reported a further enhancement of its communications capabilities. This was the introduction, in January 1977, of the Consolidated Quote System (CQS). This made possible the integration into a single presentation of bid-and-ask quotes—the market information that previously had been separately quoted on the exchanges and by third marketmakers: the broker-dealers who were not members of the exchanges, but who were making markets in listed stocks away from the exchanges.

Obviously embarrassed again by the Cinderella-like transformation of the OTC market from insignificance to its leadership role in securities industry technology, the New York Stock Exchange launched in April 1978, the Intermarket Trading System (ITS). It began on a pilot basis between the Big Board and the Philadelphia Stock Exchange. By August, the Pacific Stock Exchange, the Boston Stock Exchange, the Midwest Stock Exchange, and the American Stock Exchange also were participating in ITS.

In its 1978 annual report, the New York Stock Exchange described the development of ITS as "a signal accomplishment by the six independent market centers who put aside individual concerns to serve the overriding interests of investors and the capital markets." The annual report continued, "Soon after the introduction of ITS, another element of the National Market System came on line. Beginning August 1, stockbrokers and their customers were able to obtain, through the Consolidated Quote System, bid and asked price quotations, with size, from all market centers where listed stocks are traded."

Some readers of the above found it difficult to believe the organization issuing this annual report was the same New York Stock Exchange that had bitterly opposed the Reform Act of 1975 on the grounds that unfettered competition, the keystone to establishing a national market system, would be "the rack and ruin of the securities industry."

When the Big Board uses such complicated language as, "Soon after the introduction of ITS, another element of the National Market System came on line.... the Consolidated Quote System," in an effort to rewrite recent history, the net effect is to convince objective observers (journalists, academicians, legislators, investors-at-large, etc.) that the New York Stock Exchange in reality has become more of an antic clown than an industry leader.

The CQS "came on line" because it was developed, not by the Big Board, but by the same people who created NASDAQ. The ITS, rather than being "another element of the National Market System," was described in the *Wall Street Journal* by a top official of one of the nation's largest securities firms as "a tom-tom compared to a communications satellite" in terms of what is really needed to develop a national market system. The proportion of total volume transactions handled by ITS is pitifully small.

Occasionally one of the old guard supporters of the status quo gets the "new religion," i.e., that the chief impediment to structuring a national market system is not technological inadequacy, but human inflexibility or refusal to compromise.

Some Big Board diehards reportedly were extremely frustrated and disconcerted when they encountered the following report in *Securities Week*:

> "Goldman Sachs principal John Whitehead, in a rare stand for a senior Wall Street official, recently told the SEC that the 1975 unfixing of commission rates has improved the capital markets. During recent testimony at the agency's hearings on NASD syndicate practice rules, Whitehead acknowledged in response to questions from Commissioner Irv Pollack, 'It is probably true that the markets with unfixed commissions are more efficient than they were with fixed commissions.'"

TWO QUESTIONS FOR THE NYSE

"Improving the capital markets" should be the goal, of course, of all elements of the securities industry in response to the nation's overriding need for huge capital investments to improve productivity.

Indeed, that is the widely heralded goal of the Securities Reform Act of 1975. Since the New York Stock Exchange fulfills such a key role in this basic and vital segment of our economy, two foundational questions deserve careful examination. The first is, How hard has the Big Board been working at helping to build a national market system?

A National Market System

The Exchange's response to this question seems to be to point to the Intermarket Trading System. In 1979, the ITS accounted for 2.26 percent of total shares traded—four years after the creation of a national market system was mandated by law. Again, the technology already is available for a highly-automated and cost-efficient trading system. This has been clearly demonstrated by the Cincinnati Stock Exchange that already has such a system in operation.

One reason why the Big Board has managed to preserve its privileged status over the years has been its ability to identify and destroy potential competitors. The fully-automated Cincinnati exchange has been evaluated by securities experts as the wave-of-the-future trading system. Among its supporters have been such muscular firms as Merrill Lynch and Paine Webber.

Sharpening its ax, the NYSE moved forcefully to end the threat from the upstart Cincinnati exchange. The Big Board submitted to the SEC a blistering criticism in mid-1978 of its youthful competitor. To the Big Board, the electronic structure in Cincinnati, functioning without such NYSE components as trading posts, specialists, and throngs of stockbrokers doing their thing on the exchange floor, was an arrow aimed straight at the heart of the NYSE.

The arguments advanced by the Big Board against the Cincinnati exchange were so foolish that the SEC was moved to characterize them publicly as "bizarre." The supervisory agency also added that it was "heartened" by the increasing support of the Cincinnati system in the securities industry.

If the NASD can come up with such technological advances as NASDAQ and CQS, and if Cincinnati can change to a fully-automated system, then shouldn't one expect something more than a tom-tom from the New York Exchange, if it has a true commitment to building a fully competitive national market system?

Obviously, the Big Board's chief commitment is fighting a rear guard action against the forces of change rather than exercising a leadership role in helping the securities industry cope with such challenges.

The second question is, What can the New York Stock Exchange do to help improve the capital formation system?

Unfortunately, not much, in view of its commitment to preserve its residual privileges of the past. But it could make a substantial contribution if it were to change its policy from defensive reaction to constructive action in meeting the need for a competitive national market system.

Rule 390

The NYSE could take a giant step in this direction by dismantling—voluntarily—such archaic, anticompetitive devices as Rule 390.

As originally concocted, Rule 390 prohibited Big Board member firms from trading issues listed on the Exchange elsewhere than at the Exchange. Since the Reform Act of 1975, there have been several modifications of Rule 390, none of them of much significance. The modification most widely heralded by the Exchange has been the exemption of several hundred listed stocks, now traded via the Intermarket Trading System—an excellent example of an elephant laboring to bring forth a mouse.

Why has the New York Stock Exchange been permitted to continue to hide behind Rule 390, given the anticompetitive mandates of the 1975 Act?

At first, meaning immediately following the 1975 Act, an argument could be made to delay the elimination of Rule 390 until a computerized automated marketplace, including a Consolidated Limit Order Book (CLOB), could be designed. The validity of this argument has been shattered by the advent of the Cincinnati trading system.

According to Robert A. Swinarton, formerly vice chairman, Dean Witter Reynolds Inc., the rest of the arguments advanced in support of retention of Rule 390 were based mainly on assumptions: that markets would become fragmented and decentralized; or that the capital-raising mechanism would be destroyed. Assumptions also were advanced as compelling arguments for retaining Rule 390 on grounds that its elimination would *destroy* competition. If there is a familiar ring to these assumptions, it is because we heard it all during the controversy over unfixing rates. The SEC properly monitored advent of competitive rates and presumably could and would have intervened if any of the above horrors had materialized. The SEC should employ the same procedure in the removal of Rule 390. Why should we speculate on assumptions when we can have a true, meaningful test that will not involve commitment of dollars nor negate opportunity of anyone to compete or exist? Why should not monitored removal of Rule 390 be the ultimate in testing the speculative assumptions?

Congress, which could force the SEC to act if it so chose, for the most part has been inactive since 1975.

WHAT ABOUT THE FUTURE?

Can the auction process contribute significantly to the capital-formation needs of the next decades? Will a national market system effectively get off the ground? Will the securities marketplaces truly respond in the public interest?

As the financial capital of this country, Wall Street—in its generic sense—always will be a key component of its money markets, regardless of what shape the new NMS begins to assume.

A new generation of investment community leaders already have begun to take the reins. They have opened new markets—in options, financial futures, in money market funds, in tax-advantaged investments. It will be this generation that will design the new marketplaces and mobilize the new technology to get the job done.

If the auction markets—symbolized by the Big Board—can prove they function in the public interest, there indeed will be a role for them. They will have to prove their usefulness in the traditional testing laboratory that has made the free enterprise economy of the United States one of the greatest wonders of human history. That testing process takes place in the crucible of competition.

The securities industry generally, and the auction markets particularly, are in the agonizing struggle of massive changes. Change brings both problems and opportunities. The problems will be solved because they *must* be solved; they are essentially human problems and as such they will be resolved by human creativity.

Opportunities in the securities industry never have been, and probably never will be again, more numerous and potentially more rewarding than they are in the decade now underway.

Overleaf: Increased opportunities for women and minorities are available in the securities industry. Training programs rely heavily on intensive course work and on-the-job orientation sessions.

CHAPTER 10

GETTING STARTED AND GETTING AHEAD

In many fields, a large part of the challenge of success is actually gaining entry. Acceptance into medical school or law school alone does not guarantee you will become an outstanding attorney or physician. However, in a certain sense, it does represent entry to those professions, since you can't get started at all without the prerequisite educational credentials for these professions.

PATHS OF ENTRY

The securities industry is different. There are many separate facets of the industry, and the routes to entry are just as varied. But there is no single school, no single apprenticeship, no single "good connection" that can assure a swift lift to the top as an investment banker, bond trader, or account executive. It's on-the-job performance that alone opens the door to success in the securities industry.

Landing a position on Wall Street is no sure thing by any means. Given normal intelligence, however, and sufficient desire—and a bit of luck doesn't hurt—you should be able to find a place in the securities business.

"A journey of 10,000 miles begins with a single step," wrote a Chinese sage many years ago. And, of course, it is still true. But what should be your first step toward a career on Wall Street after leaving school?

Establish a Connection

Despite all that may have been said about how all-important it is to have attended the "right college," the fact remains that the best way to find a position on Wall Street is to know someone, or to get to know someone, in the industry.

No matter who you are, you can "connect" in the investment business. It may be a relative, a friend of a friend, or a friend of a friend of a friend. But if you try hard enough, someone will be willing to sit down with you and talk about the securities business.

The next step is to show your connection your resumé. Your inside "contact" can advise you on the strength of your qualifications and help you see the manager responsible for the desired position. At the very least, you will be sure the right people have seen your resumé.

Wall Street is a people-to-people business. And it should be no surprise that the largest number of new entrants originates as personal references.

Here are a few true-to-life examples of how some people have gotten started:

Barbara Johnson, a municipal bond trader, received a call one hectic afternoon from her cousin. Her cousin told her of a friend, Susan French, who wanted to work in the securities business. Barbara mentioned that she was very busy but said she would get in touch.

Some time later, on a slow trading day, Barbara called Susan and set up an appointment for her to visit the firm. When Susan arrived, Barbara learned she had spent the last two years working in the credit department of a local bank and had an undergraduate degree in marketing.

Barbara arranged for Susan to talk with the recruiter for her firm's sales training program and introduced her as a friend. The recruiter liked the combination of Susan's educational background and practical experience; he was also favorably impressed by Susan's poise during the interview.

Two months later, Susan French entered the securities firm as a trainee.

The major advantage of the "Know Someone" method is that it saves a good deal of time. It can put you and your resumé next to the hiring decision-maker quickly and in a positive context. If you are not hired on the first try, don't give up. The contact on the inside probably has friends at other securities firms where there may be an opening.

Have a Graduate Degree in Business Administration

An MBA degree from an accredited graduate school of business administration provides great promise for entry into a major securities firm. Since the major firms launched vast expansion programs in their investment banking, syndicate, and corporate finance departments in the seventies, the sources that they have been canvassing first have been the major graduate schools of business administration.

This is not to say that the firms draw solely from graduate schools. Far from it; but a degree from one of these schools carries considerable weight on Wall Street. When there are only a limited number of places for new entrants to be filled, the majority of them will go to graduates of business schools.

A graduate degree in business administration tells a securities firm several things about you: First, that you have the aptitude and grounding in the basic skills Wall Street is looking for; second, that you are serious about your career in business; third, that you are familiar with the latest techniques in the business world, and fourth, that your degree will command respect from the clients of the firm.

Each year, almost all big sell side firms send representatives to places like Harvard, Stanford, and Wharton to screen candidates for employment. Last year, Ron Barrows, a Harvard second-year MBA student, interviewed five of the firms. In one case, he spoke with a junior partner at one of the nation's most well-known investment banking houses who impressed him very favorably. Of the five firms at which he interviewed, two made offers, and one was the investment banking house he liked. This year, he is an associate in the Special Purpose Financing Department of that firm at an annual salary of $26,000.

Not everyone goes to the well-known business schools; even so, an MBA from almost any school will help you interview with a securities firm. However, the fact remains that, at the entry level, the more prestigious the graduate school of business, the faster—and wider—the doors will open.

Gain On-the-Job Experience

Even though one lacks impressive educational credentials, there are other points of entry into the securities business. On-the-job experience in sales, marketing, accounting, banking, and in personnel are all valuable related backgrounds for the securities business. In particular, sales jobs in a financially-related field will make securities firm personnel look twice at your resumé. Experience either in the working world, in the military, or in graduate school is almost mandatory.

Another case history will illustrate this. At the age of twenty-seven, Mike Ryan was disenchanted with accounting. His monotonous routine as a junior corporate auditor did not fulfill his need for excitement, change, or the challenge of making split-second decisions. On the advice of a friend, he advertised in "The Blue List"—the daily trade publication listing municipal bond offerings—describing himself as an accountant seeking a place in the bond business.

After about three weeks, Mike had received requests for interviews from seven firms. He was offered a position by one of them at $15,000 per year. Today after three years in the business, Mike is very busy, very excited, and earns $34,000 per year.

Never underestimate the power of good fortune—and recognizing it when it comes along. Being at the right place at the right time with the right skills means going out to meet opportunity without waiting for it to knock at your door. In most situations, good fortune boils down to a case of effort and persistence.

DESIRABLE PERSONAL CHARACTERISTICS

Once you have determined how you are going to gain entry into the securities business, you ought to be aware of what kind of individual characteristics a Wall Street firm looks for in its potential employees. The various personal, character, and personality traits one securities firm prizes most highly in an individual may be different in another firm. There may be differences, too, depending on the position to be filled. The requirements for an associate in a corporate finance department, for instance, will differ from those for a clerk in the operations department. In general, however, Wall Street firms prefer individuals who demonstrate the following characteristics.

Convey Trust

A Wall Street job candidate should be generally conservative in appearance and deportment. The securities industry trades in two important commodities—trust and money. To a great extent, trust is based on your appearance and the way you relate to people.

For their corporate finance departments, securities firms want to hire individuals whose demeanor in their mid-twenties will permit them to communicate effectively with chief financial officers who often are in their mid-fifties. The importance of the ability to interview well, to be articulate and self-assured, cannot be overstated.

Have the Proper Fit

A Wall Street intangible closely related to appearance and demeanor is the question of "fit." In almost any field, firms are reluctant to hire persons they do not think will fit, but the securities industry in particular considers this attribute crucial. "Looking right" is so important, in fact, that given two people with relatively equal qualifications, the person who appears to fit better will get the job. The question of fit is there, it is real, and if you want to work on Wall Street, you should regard it as important.

Communicate Well

In many ways, the securities business is a business of communications. Above-average verbal and written communications skills are required every day on Wall Street by individuals who must tell the rest of their firm, their customers, and frequently other firms, precisely what is going on in a specific transaction. In corporate finance, in sales, in the syndicate department, and in trading and operations, the need is the same: to communicate frequently, swiftly, and accurately. Wall Street indeed is a people-to-people business; people working together have to communicate with each other effectively.

Most jobs in the securities industry will put you in contact with other people every day. The ability to "get along," therefore, is no less important than the ability to communicate. If you have always looked wistfully at the solitude of the forest ranger, most probably the securities business is not for you.

Handle Pressures with Ease

Most Wall Street positions (notably securities trading, corporate finance, sales, and syndicate work) generate intense pressure.

Often, millions of dollars can be riding on one deal. The success or failure of that one deal can hinge on making a key decision at precisely the right time. An account executive can make or lose thousands of dollars for his customers in a single telephone call. A bond trader can "dump a bundle" in a single trade—or make one. The importance of encountering such pressures with ease cannot be overstated. Peace descends on the securities business only on Sundays and national holidays.

Be Thorough with Details

You may have heard some business executive say, "I never do paperwork; that's just a detail." Rest assured that that individual does not work in the securities business. In a large sense, the securities business *is* detail. There are forms and other details to be attended to every time a security is traded. Getting the fine print right in a prospectus and the setting up of a "road show" to introduce a new stock offering both require meticulous attention to detail. At the entry level, a major part of the job can be checking these details.

The attributes mentioned above are ideals. No one working on Wall Street has all of them to the fullest extent. They do represent qualities that have helped others to succeed in the securities business. In considering a career on Wall Street, you ought to carefully take stock of yourself to see how well you measure up.

SUGGESTED AREAS TO CONSIDER

The sweeping changes that have overtaken Wall Street since May 1, 1975, have had a significant impact on the types of positions in demand today in the securities industry. The advent of modern full-service securities firms has caused contraction in some positions and expansion in others.

The change from the partnership as the primary mode of Wall Street management to the publicly-held corporation has led to the

Marketing

Marketing, a discipline virtually unknown on Wall Street twenty years ago, is now a flourishing field. The rise of new investment vehicles, such as unit trust funds, liquid assets funds, and government-agency securities, requires marketing professionals to advise account executives on the most effective way to sell these products to the public.

Communications

Communications is another job category that has expanded with the rise of the large, full-service securities firms. These firms daily turn out reports on new products, companies, markets, and personnel changes. The ability to design and write professional, coherent reports or top quality investment advisory guidelines increasingly will be in demand on Wall Street.

Sales

To a considerable extent, the added expenses involved in larger staffs for larger firms have been met by the expansion of the sales forces. The demand for the consistent revenue producer has never been higher on Wall Street. The expansion of the sales force has caused an increased emphasis on sales training programs—and on competent training personnel as well.

Public Relations and Advertising

Keener competition since 1975 has also resulted in expansion of the public relations and advertising arms of the major securities firms. In order to expand and hold market share, especially at the retail level, firms are spending millions of dollars for time and space in various advertising media. Public relations is equally useful in publicizing the investment services available to the securities firm's clients, actual and potential.

Personnel Management

Personnel management is another growing area on Wall Street. Many firms now realize that it takes personnel professionals to attract and hold competent employees over the long haul.

Securities Analysts and Finance Officers

Perhaps the longest casualty list resulting from the recent tidal wave of Wall Street mergers has been that of the securities analysts. Today there are scores of competent analysts without jobs, and the number of positions available shrinks almost daily. There will always be a demand for effective and competent security analysis. However, because of the severe contraction in the number of positions available, only the top qualified candidates should hope for success at the entry level.

This same pattern of contraction has taken place in corporate finance departments, syndicate departments, compliance departments, and other areas where mergers have created position redundancies. Although there are positions available on Wall Street in these areas, the supply lately has been outpacing demand.

COMPENSATION LEVELS

Compensation is the basic reason why most of us work. On an average, compensation in the securities industry equals—and usually exceeds—any other industry in the U.S. economy. The days are over, however, when a rich family could insure the future wealth of an offspring by purchasing a seat on the New York Stock Exchange. Nevertheless, most securities industry employees can be sure of a good salary compared to the national averages. And some *might* strike it rich.

Ranging Upward

Corporate finance, sales, syndication, securities analysis, and trading are the highest paid enterprises in the securities industry. Sales, as an aggregate revenue-producer, ranks first simply because there are more people making money in sales than anywhere else.

In some securities firms, it is not unusual to see a well-seasoned account executive earn more each year than the $250,000 chairman of the company. The reason for this is simple: the more you sell, the more you make. A sales veteran with a healthy collection of affluent accounts can bring in as much as $750,000 a year to his firm in commission income. With most securities firms paying the account executive about 33 percent of the gross commissions, this gives the salesman a before-tax income of $250,000.

A word of caution: by no means do all securities salesmen make that much money. To be a producer in the $200,000-plus bracket requires hard work, good analytical skills, and the ability to inspire trust. Most of all, it requires effectiveness in producing positive results for customers. A top salesperson does not remain a top salesperson for long without keeping customers satisfied.

The average securities salesperson, with a minimum of five years in the business, earns about $50,000 per year. The first three or so years can be very lean ones indeed, however.

Most firms will underwrite the first-year efforts of the recently graduated sales trainee with what is known as a draw—in effect, an advance against commissions generated. This usually ranges from between $15,000 and $22,000 per year depending on your qualifications and experience. If you produce less than your draw for the first two years, or are underperforming in other ways, most firms will suggest tactfully that you begin examining other career opportunities.

One last note on compensation in the sales end of the securities business: it is cyclical. Like farming—or indeed the rest of the economy—Wall Street has its lean years and its years of plenty. Most Wall Street salespeople become amateur economists, keeping a weather eye on key indicators. And for good reason; more than in most professions, economic swings determine the size of their paychecks.

The compensation paid to entry-level corporate finance associates rivals closely the salaries paid to associates in top-flight law firms. The average starting salary for an associate in 1979 was about $24,000.

As one gains experience and rank, the salaries grow commensurately higher. The average compensation of the head of large corporate finance departments can rival that of corporate presidents in other industries.

Like sales or corporate finance, salaries in securities trading at its upper levels is almost open ended. Traders' salaries generally start between $15-$20,000. Then, after about four years in the business, a trader can be earning as much as $50,000. A more likely average is between $35,000 and $40,000; top salaries can exceed $100,000.

Most Wall Streeters agree that, although the peaks for high-salaried security analysts have been reached, the salaries of those who remain in the business are quite good. The average analyst earns between $40,000 and $50,000 per year. And some—those who consistently achieve superstar status—can make more than $100,000.

Technicians and Technologists

The advent of the computer to Wall Street has caused a rise in salaries in the operations departments of most Wall Street firms.

Operational efficiency is of vital importance as trading volume continues to mount, and accounting errors become more damaging to profits. Firms are willing to pay competitive salaries for technicians and technologists who can minimize these error rates—those who can design and operate the sophisticated electronic data processing and other automated systems without which, because of the huge increases in volume, the securities industry would be paralyzed.

Wall Street—like the rest of America—smiles on education. When you interview for a position at a securities firm, ask about the tuition assistance plan. Major firms have them and will reimburse employees for business-related courses. Some firms will even pay for the entire cost of an MBA. Other courses, investment seminars, speaker training, sales techniques and lately, computer programming, are also beneficial to an individual's long term career. They're readily available for those who are qualified.

Business education has one pragmatic goal: to help you produce. No matter what area you are involved in on Wall Street, you are judged by results. Results in the securities business translate into dollar income for the firm. Therefore, the volume of production in sales, corporate finance, syndication, securities trading, or operations is the single greatest key to advancement in the securities business.

PLACEMENT AND ADVANCEMENT OF WOMEN

The opportunities for advancement are increasing rapidly for women in the securities industry. While it is true that Wall Street traditionally has been a male-dominated industry—and in fact still is—there is every indication that the decade of the 1980s will be the "Decade of the Woman" in the securities industry.

The total working population on Wall Street, meaning all phases of the securities industry, stands at about 500,000. Women hold more than one-third of the jobs in sell side and buy side organizations. But less than seven percent are in management or professional-level positions. Between 1974 and 1979 the number of women directors on the boards of leading Wall Street firms increased from four to twelve.

The first women in professional positions on Wall Street were security analysts, hired in the early 1960s to cover cosmetics, retailing, and other consumer industries. As the demand for analysts grew during the boom years of that decade, management found that these women could cover heavy machinery, banks, aviation, and other industries as well as men.

Securities firms have increased their efforts to hire more women at the management and professional levels in the seventies. Many women now have responsible positions as corporate finance associates and account executives. Some have approached superstar status in terms of earnings.

There seems to be evidence that, since the Equal Employment Opportunity Commission has appeared on the scene, Wall Street has been making a definite effort to hire more women account executives. This regulating body may well provide additional impetus to accelerate the trend as securities firms seek to avoid the possible imposition of tough quota rules.

Although women are now getting better jobs at better pay on Wall Street, it genuinely is only the beginning. As the old days' last vestiges disappear, modern securities firms increasingly are offering new opportunities and new career paths right to the top.

CONCLUSION

It is difficult to advise someone precisely of the best way of making a contact, what positions in the securities industry will be expanding and contracting in the future, or where an opening may be at any given time. But to a great degree, the dynamics of change are part and parcel of the excitement and challenge of Wall Street.

The number of jobs available each year is largely a function of the marketplace. And that market is highly volatile—changing and growing day-to-day. One thing is certain, there will always be a Wall Street, and there will always be room there for the talented individual who finds the investment business a challenging and exciting venture.

APPENDIX A

GLOSSARY OF SECURITIES TERMS

Arbitrageur. A dealer in stock who simultaneously purchases or sells shares in merger/acquisition situations in order to reduce fluctuation and help maintain negotiable prices.

Bear Market. A market influenced by widespread belief that prices will decline.

Bond Indenture. The contract under which bonds are issued, setting such terms as rate of interest, payment dates, conversion privileges, and other conditions.

Bond Price Quotation. The percent of par (the face value of the bond) at which the bond is quoted. Thus, 90 means 90 percent (for a $1,000 par value bond, this would be $900). Similarly, 110 would mean 110 percent of par, or $1,100 on a $1,000 bond.

Call. See *Option.*

Capital Gain or Loss. Profit (or loss) from the sale of securities (or real estate), considered as capital assets. Income tax laws define a short-term capital gain as acquired in 12 months or less, and a long-term capital gain as one from assets held longer than one year.

Capitalization. The total amount of the various securities issued by a corporation, including bonds, debentures, preferred and common stock, and surplus.

Commercial Paper. Corporate IOU's issued for repayment over short-term periods up to 270 days. Most frequently issued through dealers by leading utility, industrial, or finance companies. Some large financial companies issue commercial paper directly. Common denomination is $100,000.

Commodity, Commodities Trading. One of approximately fifty agricultural products, minerals, or raw materials traded at approximately twelve exchanges either for cash or by contract specifying dates and amounts for future exchange.

Common Shares. Shares stipulating part ownership in a company, with voting privileges and claims to earnings, dividends, and assets in event of liquidation.

Convertible Debt Issues. Bonds of a corporation issued for sale, offering the investor the safety of a straight investment, with the added possibility of profit through stipulated conditions on which the investment may be converted to stock or some similar privilege.

Debenture. A promissory note of debt that is backed by the general credit of the issuing company, usually a manufacturing or industrial firm, and usually not secured by a property lien or a mortgage.

Debt Issues. Bonds, notes, or other types of securities for which the holder receives interest and the principal of which is repaid to the holder upon maturity.

Equity (or Stockholders' Equity). Shareowners' ownership interest in a company represented by their common and preferred stock.

ERISA. The Employee Retirement Income Security Act. This act, which was passed by Congress in 1974, supersedes the state-administered pension trust laws. It requires prudent investment of pension funds to insure optimum financial returns and full disclosure to employees of how pension funds are being managed. It enlarges tax-exempt provisions for the self-employed who must finance their own pension plans and provides for tax-sheltered retirement pools for individuals.

Fannie Maes. Mortgages sold by the prime lender to the Federal National Mortgage Association, whose credit is guaranteed by the government.

Ginnie Maes. Mortgages for lower-income housing, mainly Federal Housing Authority insured multi-family projects, sold by the prime lender to the Government National Mortgage Association.

Gross National Product. The aggregate market value of a country's final output of goods and services. Commonly referred to as the GNP.

Hedging. Means of making sales contracts in advance at current prices to protect against loss due to price fluctuations.

Investment Banking. The process whereby a securities firm buys part or all of a securities issue from a corporation or government body for resale to individuals or institutions. Two or more investment bankers may combine to do this. (See *Syndicate.*)

Investment Banking Syndicate. See *Syndicate.*

Load. A commission charged to the buyer of most mutual fund shares, which takes care of sales, promotion, and distribution costs.

Long-term Debt. The capital securities of a company, meaning bonds and debentures that have maturities of more than one year.

Margin. Money given a stockbroker by one on whose account a purchase or sale is to be made as security against loss.

Mortgage Bonds. Bonds that are secured by a mortgage on real estate property and usually classified according to their priority of claim against the property. Corporate bonds are in this category.

Municipal Bonds. Bonds issued by cities and towns to finance major expenditures; for example, general obligation bonds, housing authority tax bonds, revenue bonds, etc.

Mutual Fund. A company that purchases and manages a portfolio of market securities for the benefit of its shareholders.

NASD. The National Association of Securities Dealers, Inc. An organization of brokers and dealers set up to supervise the over-the-counter segment of the securities industry; to adopt, administer, and enforce the rules of fair practice and industry ethics; and to prevent fraud and market manipulation.

NASDAQ. National Association of Securities Dealers Automated Quotations. An automated system that uses an electronic quote board (with hook-ups to member offices) to show the current prices of securities.

Option. A purchased contractual right to buy (referred to as a call) or to sell (referred to as a put) 100 shares of a particular stock at a particular price by a particular date. The contract obliges the purchaser to buy the stock at the specified price (if a call) or to deliver it (if a put), if the value of the shares moves in the opposite direction, or even holds steady, the purchaser loses the amount he paid for the option.

Over-the-counter (OTC). That segment of the securities industry where securities not listed on any exchange are traded between dealers who act as principals or as brokers for customers. The trading is done by bargaining or negotiation, usually by telephone, as contrasted with the auction bid system used in the exchanges. The OTC market is the main market for municipal and U.S. Government bonds.

Par. The face value of a bond or preferred stock; as applied to common stock, the dollar value of a share as stated in the company's charter.

Pass-throughs. Investment vehicles consisting mostly of Fannie Maes and Ginnie Maes packaged as secondary mortgage bundles sold by mortgage bankers to institutional investors as long-term investments.

Preferred Shares. Shares that stipulate the right to a company's earnings and assets prior to the claim of common shares.

Prospectus. An official printed statement that must be furnished to prospective purchasers of new securities listed with the

Securities and Exchange Commission. It must fully disclose the company's property, the business engaged in, the prospects for the future of the company, its competition, the nature of the security offered, how the proceeds will be used, the history of the company, the background of the management, and certified financial statements.

Put. See *Option.*

Registered Competitive Marketmaker. As of May 1, 1978, a member of a special category of Exchange members charged with maintaining a fair and orderly market in the open bidding by making a bid or an offer if asked by a floor official or by a floor broker holding an unexpected customer's order.

Revenue Bonds. Tax-exempt securities issued by a local or state authority.

Securities. Common stock, preferred stock, bonds, and warrants that have been issued by a corporation or government agency.

Securities and Exchange Commission (SEC). The government agency created by Congress in 1934 to administer the Securities Act of 1933 and the Securities Exchange Act of 1934 as well as many laws enacted since then. This organization helps protect investors.

Selling Short. Instructing your broker to sell stock before purchase in hope that you will acquire it at a lower price than that of the delivery price.

Syndicate. A group of investment banks that jointly underwrite and distribute a new issue of securities or a large holding of stock of an outstanding issue. The union is only for that particular issue, although the banks may join on other issues from time to time. (See *Underwriters.*)

Underwriters. Investment bankers who underwrite (or guarantee the sale of) an issue of corporate or government securities. Underwriters either buy the issue and sell it to investors through their own organization, or form a syndicate to help dispose of the securities. (See *Syndicate.*)

Warrant. A negotiable security (issued by a company) that represents a long-term option to purchase common stock from the company on specified terms.

Yield. The proceeds or returns from an investment. These dividends or interest paid by a company are expressed as a percentage of the current price.

APPENDIX B

FOR FURTHER INFORMATION

Here are the names and addresses of some securities industry groups that can supply you with more information on various aspects of the securities industry.

American Bankers Association
1120 Connecticut Avenue, N.W.
Washington, D.C. 20036

American Finance Association
New York University—GBA
100 Trinity Place
New York, New York 10006

American Institute of Certified
  Public Accountants
1211 Avenue of the Americas
New York, New York 10036

Association of Investment Brokers
44 Beaver Street—Suite 405
New York, New York 10004

Financial Analysts Federation
219 East 42 Street
New York, New York 10017

Financial Women's Association of
  New York
P. O. Box 949
Wall Street Association
New York, New York 10005

Investment Counsel Association
  of America, Inc.
127 East 59 Street
New York, New York 10022

National Association of Securities
  Dealers, Inc.
1735 K Street, N.W.
Washington, D.C. 20006

National Security Traders
  Association
55 Broad Street
New York, New York 10004

Securities Industry Association
20 Broad Street
New York, New York 10005

Registered Securities Exchanges in the United States

American Stock Exchange, Inc.
86 Trinity Place
New York, New York 10006

Chicago Board Options Exchange
 (CBOE)
141 West Jackson Boulevard
Chicago, Illinois 60604

Midwest Stock Exchange
120 South LaSalle Street
Chicago, Illinois 60603

New York Stock Exchange, Inc.
11 Wall Street
New York, New York 10005

VGM CAREER HORIZONS SERIES

CAREER PLANNING
How to Land a Better Job
How to Write a Winning Résumé
Life Plan
Planning Your College Education
Planning your Military Career

SURVIVAL GUIDES
High School Survival Guide
College Survival Guide

OPPORTUNITIES IN
Available in both paperback and hardbound editions
Accounting Careers
Acting Careers
Advertising Careers
Airline Careers
Animal and Pet Care
Appraising Valuation Science
Architecture
Automotive Service
Banking
Beauty Culture
Biological Sciences
Book Publishing
Broadcasting Careers
Building Construction Trades
Cable Television
Carpentry
Chemical Engineering
Chemistry
Chiropractic Health Care
Civil Engineering
Commercial Art and Graphic Design
Computer Science Careers
Counseling & Guidance
Dance
Data Processing Careers
Dental Care
Drafting Careers
Electrical Trades
Electronic and Electrical Engineering
Energy Careers
Engineering Technology
Environmental Careers
Fashion
Federal Government Careers
Film Careers
Financial Careers
Fire Protection Services
Food Services
Foreign Language Careers
Forestry Careers
Free Lance Writing
Government Service
Graphic Communications
Health and Medical Careers
Hospital Administration
Hotel & Motel Management
Industrial Design
Interior Design
Journalism Careers
Landscape Architecture
Law Careers
Law Enforcement and Criminal Justice
Library and Information Science
Machine Shop Trades
Magazine Publishing
Management
Marine & Maritime
Materials Science
Mechanical Engineering
Microelectronics
Modeling Careers
Music Careers
Nursing Careers
Occupational Therapy
Office Occupations
Opticianry
Optometry
Packaging Science
Paralegal Careers
Paramedical Careers
Personnel Management
Pharmacy Careers
Photography
Physical Therapy
Podiatric Medicine
Printing Careers
Psychiatry
Psychology
Public Relations Careers
Real Estate
Recreation and Leisure
Refrigeration and Air Conditioning
Religious Service
Sales & Marketing
Secretarial Careers
Securities Industry
Sports & Athletics
Sports Medicine
State and Local Governm
Teaching Careers
Technical Communications
Telecommunications
Theatrical Design & Production
Transportation
Travel Careers
Veterinary Medicine
Word Processing
Writing Careers
Your Own Service Busine

WOMEN IN
Available in both paperback and hardboun editions
Communications
Engineering
Finance
Government
Management
Science
Their Own Business

 VGM Career Horizons
A Division of National Textbook Company
4255 West Touhy Avenue
Lincolnwood, Illinois 60646-1975 U.S.A.